THE EVERYTHING
PARENT'S GUIDE TO

RAISING A GIFTED CHILD

Dear Reader,

This book is a compilation of all the research I have done, knowledge I have gained, and wisdom I have gleaned over the last thirty years as a gifted student and gifted educator. I hope that this information can help you better understand and parent your gifted child.

Parenting a gifted child is no easy task. You face long hours, exhausting emotional behaviors, and endless repetitions of the question "Why?" You might feel like there is no one to turn to who understands what you are going through. My hope is that reading this book will feel like turning to a friend for advice and suggestions as you make those difficult choices parents of gifted children so often face.

The greatest single piece of advice I can give any gifted parent is advice once given to me as a teacher: "Remember that a child's giftedness provides an explanation for why they are the way they are, but it is never an excuse." With this book, I hope to help you see how you can have a fuller picture of who your child is in order to train him wisely as a parent to reach his full potential.

Your partner in the journey,

Sarah Herbert Robbins, MEd

WELCOME TO THE

EVERYTHING®
PARENT'S GUIDES

Everything® Parent's Guides are a part of the bestselling Everything® series and cover common parenting issues like childhood illnesses and tantrums, as well as medical conditions like asthma and juvenile diabetes. These family-friendly books are designed to be a one-stop guide for parents. If you want authoritative information on specific topics not fully covered in other books, Everything® Parent's Guides are your perfect solution.

Alerts

Urgent warnings

Facts

Important snippets of information

Essentials

Quick handy tips

Questions

Answers to common questions

When you're done reading, you can finally say you know **EVERYTHING®**!

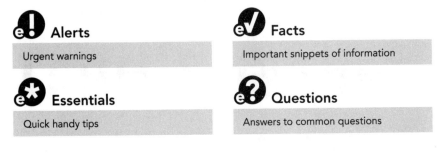

PUBLISHER Karen Cooper

DIRECTOR OF ACQUISITIONS AND INNOVATION Paula Munier

MANAGING EDITOR, EVERYTHING® SERIES Lisa Laing

COPY CHIEF Casey Ebert

ASSISTANT PRODUCTION EDITOR Melanie Cordova

ACQUISITIONS EDITOR Kate Powers

SENIOR DEVELOPMENT EDITOR Brett Palana-Shanahan

EDITORIAL ASSISTANT Ross Weisman

EVERYTHING® SERIES COVER DESIGNER Erin Alexander

LAYOUT DESIGNERS Colleen Cunningham, Erin Dawson, Michelle Roy Kelly, Elisabeth Lariviere, Denise Wallace

Visit the entire Everything® series at *www.everything.com*

THE EVERYTHING

PARENT'S GUIDE TO

RAISING A GIFTED CHILD

All you need to know to meet your child's
emotional, social, and academic needs

Sarah Herbert Robbins, MEd

Avon, Massachusetts

*To my wonderful husband and partner, Mike, who makes me
laugh, try harder, and accomplish great things I could never
do alone, and to my daughter, Debby. I hope this book helps
provide information for underserved gifted children like my
husband, and makes it better for my daughter one day.*

An Everything® Series Book.
Everything® and everything.com® are registered trademarks of F+W Media, Inc.

Published by Adams Media, a division of F+W Media, Inc.
57 Littlefield Street, Avon, MA 02322 U.S.A.
www.adamsmedia.com

ISBN 10: 1-4405-2983-3
ISBN 13: 978-1-4405-2983-2
eISBN 10: 1-4405-3031-9
eISBN 13: 978-1-4405-3031-9

Printed in the United States of America.

10 9 8 7 6 5 4 3 2 1

Library of Congress Cataloging-in-Publication Data
is available from the publisher.

This publication is designed to provide accurate and authoritative information
with regard to the subject matter covered. It is sold with the understanding that
the publisher is not engaged in rendering legal, accounting, or other professional
advice. If legal advice or other expert assistance is required, the services of a
competent professional person should be sought.
  —From a *Declaration of Principles* jointly adopted by a Committee of the
American Bar Association and a Committee of Publishers and Associations

Many of the designations used by manufacturers and sellers to distinguish their
products are claimed as trademarks. Where those designations appear in this
book and Adams Media was aware of a trademark claim, the designations have
been printed with initial capital letters.

*This book is available at quantity discounts for bulk purchases.
For information, please call 1-800-289-0963.*

**All the examples and dialogues used in this book are fictional, and
have been created by the author to illustrate disciplinary situations.**

Acknowledgments

This book would not have been possible without the help of some very important people. First and foremost, this book would not be anywhere near as helpful or grammatically accurate without the help of Missy Fox and Denise Hill—thank you for taking the time to edit, discuss, and provide suggestions as battle-weary experts still in the trenches of parenting some amazing gifted children. My sister, Molly, spent hours a college student doesn't have encouraging me and helping me correct my rusty writing skills. I'm thankful for my years teaching, including the hundreds of terrific, talented kids and parents who made me laugh, taught me what it really means to be gifted, and helped me better understand how to meet the needs of all different students, all the while becoming my friends along the way.

My parents, John and Beth Herbert, continue to be some of the greatest examples of how to parent gifted children to reach their potential. My siblings, Shane, Katy, Matt, Sam, and Molly are still my favorite source for stories and examples of gifted students. I think every class I taught heard the story of "Cactus Sam" and "Molly's Terrible Day" when we discussed perseverance and resilience. A special thanks to my husband, who put up with fast food dinners, dirty clothes, and Daddy duties in order to give me time to research and write. I would like to thank my sweet daughter for her patience with a distracted mother, her encouraging smiles with sweet giggles, and her helpful nap schedule. Finally, I'm thankful to my Creator who gave me the experiences and talents to make this book possible, while teaching me humility and gratitude.

gift·ed (gif-tid) ▶ adj. Having inborn intelligence, exceptional talent, or natural ability.

Contents

Introduction

When parents hear the word "gifted" in reference to their own child, their first response can be varied. Some parents may get excited, imagining their child becoming a future president, scientist, or writer. They see their child's endless potential stretching out before them. Other parents may be skeptical. "My child? Gifted? Have you seen his bedroom?" They may doubt the test results and dismiss them, certain that this was some kind of mistake. Still another group of parents may feel overwhelmed, recognizing the weight of the task before them. They may realize the truly awesome responsibility of raising a child whose future has limitless possibilities and on whose shoulders future greatness rests.

Regardless of which category you may fall into, you are here now. You have a child who has been diagnosed as gifted, or you think you might have a child who is gifted. This book will seek to provide answers to the many questions that may be going through your mind.

This book will help you understand what it really means to be gifted, in the clinical sense of the word. Additionally, it will help you to understand the unique traits that gifted children possess. You will also learn how to meet the needs of your gifted child socially, emotionally, and academically.

While this book may not have all the answers to your many questions on raising a gifted child, it will hopefully give you a start to better understanding your wonderfully creative and talented child.

CHAPTER 1

What Does It Mean to Be Gifted?

The term "gifted" is often used in contemporary society. It can take on many different meanings, depending on the speaker as well as the audience. The purpose of this book is to look at what it truly means for a child to be termed gifted, and how that changes the way they are parented. Initially, it is important to understand the history of gifted education. That history will help you transition into understanding what it means right now in current society for a child to be gifted. Knowing where gifted education comes from can help you to better understand its current place, as well as where it is going in the future. That is a future that now includes your own child.

A History of Gifted Education

Off and on throughout history, cultures have dealt with the idea of the highly intelligent. Plato had a school for highly intelligent boys and girls as early as 380 B.C.E. The Chinese as early as the Tang Dynasty around 600 B.C.E. searched for bright children to be trained in a variety of skills. During and following the Renaissance, education grew in importance throughout Europe, particularly with Gutenberg's printing press making books and writings available to the masses. Public school systems began around the 1800s, organizing education for the masses.

Giftedness has a fairly short history in America culture. During and after colonization, Americans followed European traditions, for the most part. University educations were mostly for men, typically well born and wealthy. Around the early 1900s, though, children began to be identified as "high achieving." Two scholars are given primary credit for the early advancements in gifted education, Alfred Binet and Martin Terman.

Alfred Binet and Martin Terman

Some parents may be familiar with the name Binet, especially if their children tested into a gifted program via the Stanford-Binet test. Alfred Binet is credited with creating the first intelligence test, which stemmed from his work with developmentally disabled children in France. He created a scale for measuring their intelligence. Binet's work was revolutionary for the field of intelligence testing, and had tremendous ramifications for the field of giftedness, as well.

This scale was later modified by Stanford psychologist Martin Terman, who developed Binet's work further to create the Stanford-Binet Intelligence Scale. The scale's goal was to determine a person's mental age, an idea that has become the idea of a person's Intelligence Quotient, or IQ. The first version of the Stanford-Binet was published in 1913, and has since been revised many times. The test, in its current form, the Binet-Kamat, is still used today.

Terman was the first person documented to use the term "gifted" to refer to individuals with a high IQ. The work of Binet and Terman standardized intelligence testing and ushered in a new era for the field of gifted education. For the first time, intelligence was quantifiable.

Many tests have been developed in the years following the work of Terman; however, most find their roots in the work of these two gentlemen.

Terman continued his work studying the gifted throughout the early 1900s. In the early 1920s, Leta Hollingworth began work with a special class of gifted students in the New York public school system. This is perhaps the first class designed specifically for the gifted. The studies of Terman and Hollingworth provided the foundation for the study of gifted education.

In the 1950s, the National Association for the Gifted was founded, and the National Defense of Education Act was passed. These, combined with the space race against the Soviet Union, helped advance the cause of the gifted. As America worked collectively to be the first into outer space and on the move, many advances in education were made to ensure a nation of mathematicians, scientists, and engineers.

The Marland Report, a comprehensive study on giftedness, which also contained the first definition of what it means to be gifted, was published in 1972. Additionally, in 1974, the Office of the Gifted and Talented was recognized by the Department of Education. In 1988, the Jacob Javits Gifted and Talented Students Education Act was passed, ensuring research is done regarding gifted and talented program development; however, it did not provide any funds at the local level for school programs.

Following these events, many colleges and universities developed programs for the study of giftedness in addition to teacher training programs. Programs specifically geared toward the needs of gifted children began to appear, albeit only sporadically, across the nation.

Work continues to be done at the research level and legal level to continue the progress of learning about and providing resources for gifted students.

Gifted Versus Smart

Many parents long to hear the wonderful words, "Your child is gifted" at any of their many parent teacher conferences throughout their child's school career. Educators are prone either to toss these terms around freely or to use them loosely. Many times, they are unaware of the true definitions behind the terms "gifted" and "bright" that they use. While many students are very bright, gifted students are rare. The following sections seek to illuminate these terms as well as help parents determine into which category their child falls.

It is important to make the distinction between students that are very bright and students that are gifted. Many students are very bright, but there is a difference between being bright and being gifted. Clinically, the difference is actually quantifiable. Taking a look at a standard bell curve will help provide information to determine whether a child is bright or truly gifted.

The Bell Curve

An understanding of a standard bell curve will help develop the true definition or what it means to be gifted. When talking about a bell curve, theorists and educators commonly refer to percentiles or standard deviations. Typically, an understanding starts from the middle and works its way out. From the top of the bell curve to the first standard deviation to the left and to the right, represents the central 68.2 percent of students. That means that when students of similar age are tested, 68.2 percent will fall within this range.

Taking the bell curve from the middle and tracing out two standard deviations to the right and to the left, gives a representation of about 95 percent of the population tested.

This is where it starts to get interesting. The further away a student scores from the tip of the bell curve, the more removed a student is from the general population. Three standard deviations to either side would represent 99.5 percent. Four standard deviations to either side would show a representation of the middle 99.7 percent. Students four standards deviations to the left are in the lowest 0.003 percent, educators would determine the child to be in need of special education services. They are generally pulled from the mainstream environment and are given special services for their special needs.

Four standard deviations to the right are the highly to the profoundly gifted. Students who test in the 95th percentile are referred to as highly gifted. Students in the 99th percentile are referred to as the profoundly gifted. Rightly so; they represent a small fraction of the population. Those in the 95th percentile and greater represent roughly 5 percent of the population, while those in the 99th percentile represent a mere 1 percent.

If and when your child is tested, they will most likely tell you what percentile he falls into in reference to this bell curve. Refer back to this section to refresh yourself on what those scores actually mean.

Gifted Versus Talented

Most people have known very talented individuals in their lifetime. They have met those that possess a special and unique skill that makes them stand out amongst their peers in a specific area. Many students have these special talents. Others see their abilities and immediately assume that they must be gifted because they have such a special skill.

Others make the opposite assumption. They see a student who does not seem to have any one special skill. They see a child who fails to meet expectations, is a troublemaker, or falls asleep in class, and assume that this child could not possibly be gifted.

The trouble with giftedness is that it is a different way of thinking. You can't see inside another person's brain, which makes it terribly difficult to determine just from observation whether or not a child is gifted. Just because a child has certain talents does not make him gifted—he might just be a talented individual in one area. Just because a child does not demonstrate a special talent does not exclude him from being gifted. Be careful not to make assumptions as to whether or not a child you know is gifted before taking in all of the facts of the situation.

Creativity and Giftedness

The relationship between creativity and giftedness has been much like a pendulum swinging back and forth over the years. At various times in history, scholars have considered creativity to be a component of giftedness. Many over the years have thought that creativity and intelligence are inextricably linked. Some state that a person must have a high intelligence in order to be able to be creative. Others have claimed that creativity is in itself a type of giftedness, in the same way that students can be mathematically gifted.

Currently, most schools do not test for creativity when they test whether or not a student is gifted. Gifted testing primarily focuses on intellectual abilities, particularly in language and science. However, once students are identified as gifted, many programs work to help a gifted child develop skills to become more creative. Additionally, creativity in problem solving is very commonly addressed, and skills to enhance these abilities are typically a part of gifted programming. This is something to ask about and consider when choosing a gifted program, especially if you sense your child is very creative and would benefit from these types of services. Not all programs have components to develop creativity, but are more scholarly. Parents of students with art and musical talents should be careful to make sure these skills are nurtured in an appropriate program.

Gardner's Definition

Howard Gardner was a scholar in the middle of the 1900s who was a pioneer in studying intelligence. He came up with many theories, the most famous of which was his theory on multiple intelligences. His ideas on multiple intelligences state that people use different skills to help them solve problems. These skills can be identified and used to develop teaching strategies, and to better meet the needs of students.

These intelligences are grouped into three categories. The academic intelligences include linguistic intelligence (a proficiency with language, both written and spoken) and logical-mathematical intelligence (analyzing problems, carrying out calculations to arrive at solutions, and logically investigating problems). The following three intelligences deal with the arts: students who are musically talented, students who have bodily kinesthetic abilities (gross motor skills that make them good athletes as well as help them to use motion and their bodies for solving problems), and spatially talented students (those who are able to recognize patterns and visually estimate problems through symbols and pictures). The final two intelligences deal with relationships and are intrapersonal skills (those who understand others as well as seem to be intuitive about the thoughts and motivations of those around them—typically considered extroverts) and interpersonal skills (these children and adults are able to be introspective, understanding their own thoughts, emotions, and intentions—typically considered introverts).

Often, when asked what type of services are provided for gifted students, teachers and administrators will note the use of multiple intelligences. Many people feel that understanding multiple intelligences is the same as understanding giftedness. When asked about what it means to be gifted, parents may hear about Howard Gardner and how students can identify their area of giftedness by looking at his multiple intelligences. However, despite Gardner's research, modern perspectives on giftedness see the understanding of multiple intelligences as really more of a discussion of learning styles than an analysis of giftedness. While making sure that content is delivered in many different formats is an excellent strategy for making sure that students learn, it is not necessarily enough to meet the diverse academic needs of a gifted student.

Testing

When a child is referred to as gifted, that typically means that they have been tested through one of a variety of means. Students who are gifted have been found to be in the top 5 percent of the population, or in the top 1 percent for being profoundly gifted. Testing is an important part of the gifted process, and has many aspects to be investigated.

Why We Test

To test or not to test? That is the question that has plagued the minds of the parents of potentially gifted students for several decades. Many parents feel that they do not need a test score to tell them whether or not their child is gifted. Others feel that being tested will label their child and cause others to see them differently. Some parents feel that gifted programs are elitist and that all children will do just fine in a regular classroom where teachers are trained to meet the needs of all the students. Another possible reason why parents resist testing is fear of their child being ostracized; refraining from testing and services allows the child to develop social skills. These are just a few reasons why parents or teachers may decide not to test.

However, there are many very good reasons why students should be tested to determine if they are gifted or not. Testing provides valuable information on a child's ability to learn. That information can be used to make sure that he receives the best possible education for his abilities. Parents can use this information to advocate for the special accommodations their child needs. Additionally, testing qualifies students for a wide variety of programs and services for which they might not otherwise be eligible. Occasionally, learning disabilities are also identified through gifted testing. Areas where a student's performance does not match his ability are brought to light where an otherwise gifted student may have been compensating for them. This can result in a child finally receiving much-needed help with both his disability as well as his giftedness.

If parents suspect that their child had a learning disability, most would not hesitate to have their child tested in order to receive every possibly advantage to their academic growth and development. Parents who are concerned that their children are gifted may view testing in this same way. If you could give your child the extra help that they qualify for and need, why would you withhold that?

Types of Testing

Gifted testing comes in a variety of forms. The type of test your child takes depends primarily on where and how he is tested. By law, most schools test students in a group-testing environment at some point in their academic career. Because so many children are tested at a time, the least expensive accepted test is used. Other parents choose to have their child tested independently by a psychiatrist or through another institution. These types of testing scenarios are typically much more expensive, but can be more accurate at providing detailed information on the child. Gifted testing can cost anywhere from $200 to $700 for parents who go outside the school system. These tests are typically divided into two primary categories: IQ tests and achievement tests.

IQ Tests

IQ tests measure an individual's ability to learn. Some common types of IQ tests that you might see are the Stanford-Binet, Wechsler Intelligence Scale for Children (WISC), and the Kaufman Assessment Battery for Children (Kaufman ABC).

 Fact

The letters "IQ" stand for intelligence quotient. The term first became popular in 1905, based on the work of Alfred Binet and Theophile Simon. It refers to a simple calculation of a person's mental age divided by their chronological age then multiplied by 100. Most people have an IQ somewhere between 85 and 115. Those below are typically considered mentally handicapped, while those above 115 are typically considered gifted.

Achievement Tests

Achievement tests do just as their name describes—test for what a child can achieve based on what they already know. Several of the common achievement tests currently popular include the Woodcock-Johnson III, the Cognitive Abilities Test (Cog-At), Naglieri Non-Verbal Ability Test (NNAT), and the Otis-Lennon School Abilities Test (OLSAT).

 Essential

To learn more about the types of tests used, or to choose a test for your own child, visit *www.hoagiesgifted.org/tests.htm*. This database for parents of gifted children provides information and reviews for each of these tests as well as others.

What the Scores Mean

After your child is tested, you will receive detailed information on how he has scored. Typically, abilities-based tests will tell you at what percentile your child ranked. Students who are scored in the 95th percentile or greater on achievement tests are typically considered gifted by most program standards. Those who score in the 99th percentile are considered highly gifted. Refer back to the bell curve at the beginning of this chapter for more information on percentiles and giftedness.

Students who take an IQ test will receive an intelligence score. If a child is scored 115–129, they are considered mildly gifted. Scores of 130–144 are considered moderately gifted. Those who score 145–159 are thought to be highly gifted. A score of 160–179 is considered exceptionally gifted, and any score over 180 is determined to be profoundly gifted. Any score over 115 will typically qualify a student for a gifted program.

Behavioral Characteristics

Often, parents and teachers with experience working with the gifted can identify a child simply by observing them. The brain works in a different way with gifted students, which can cause a few "side effects" that those working with the gifted come to recognize. Some of these characteristics include:

- Has a large, advanced vocabulary.
- Makes up her own games with complex rules.
- Learns to read early, many times teaching herself.
- Asks questions and rarely settles for a simple explanation.
- Seems to have more energy, jumping from topic to topic and activity to activity.
- Is very intuitive, and understands nonverbal cues as well as sarcasm from an early age.
- Solves problems in a logical and organized manner.
- Learns information quickly, after only one or two repetitions.
- Able to reason and to solve problems, earning them the distinction "little lawyers."
- Understands cause-and-effect relationships.

❗ Alert

It is important to remember that these are not the only behaviors of gifted students. In addition, a child can be gifted and not show these behavior characteristics. This is simply a tool that some parents might find helpful in assessing their own child, and is not intended to be exhaustive or diagnostic.

Many parents find comfort in recognizing their child's abilities in the list above. It is helpful to see that other children have the same skills and abilities as their own, when, for many, their child has been isolated and alone in her development up to the point she was identified as gifted.

Parent Observational Indicators

Most parents feel their children are gifted in a general sense of the word; however, parents of the truly gifted are often very adept at identifying their child's superior abilities. In interviews and surveys, most parents of students who were determined to be gifted were able to accurately identify in advance their child's ability level in advance. Many schools and programs recognize this parent intuition and offer checklists for parents that help to identify a child. These checklists may include items for a child's academic behaviors, motivations, creativity, and leadership, among other areas.

Academic Indicators

Teachers who are well versed in gifted education can often identify gifted students based on many academic indicators. Some characteristics are evident in a child's learning behaviors. These might include an advanced vocabulary, elaborate and detailed thinking across the disciplines, very good observation skills, and always having an answer (even though the answer may not be correct).

Teachers might observe behaviors not related to classroom work as well. They may notice that a child has strong concentration in areas where he is keenly interested, likes to learn even outside the classroom content, and is intrinsically motivated to learn (self-motivated by just learning) rather than requiring bribes.

Gifted students are often natural leaders. They take opportunities to lead groups and spearhead projects. Gifted children may also tend to be in authority over others, taking on organizing and dealing out responsibilities for those working with them. Finally, they are usually very good at helping other students by clearly explaining and describing the task or the steps to be successful in a task. Teachers particularly notice this characteristic, as it is very evident in a classroom setting.

Within the classroom, teachers may notice that a gifted child is particularly creative. They include elaborate details in their answer, stories, and explanations. They are very curious about how and why things work. Gifted students are also able to think of many possible solutions to a problem, rather than one traditional solution. This can be very good in brainstorming sessions, but very taxing in mathematics lessons. Lastly, gifted students have an uncommon knack for using unusual and inventive resources to help them with a task or problem. These are some ways that teachers might witness creativity in the classroom.

While many teachers may not quickly recognize a student as gifted, when they learn behavioral characteristics such as the ones mentioned, they are typically more likely to be able to spot those special students. Teachers are often looking for a bright child who always has a right answer and is well behaved. This does not always fit the gifted mold; however, teachers can learn to use these classroom behavioral markers to become skilled at identifying gifted students even without the use of complicated testing procedures or their grade book.

🅐 Alert

Parents can offer a teacher a gifted indicator checklist if they feel that a teacher may not be fully recognizing their child's potential. When a teacher sees how many of the gifted characteristics a child is displaying, they may be more likely to recognize a child as gifted. In addition, practice using a gifted indicator checklist of some type will help teachers become more versed in identifying gifted behaviors for future students.

Teacher Observation and Recommendations

Many teachers have a preconceived understanding of what it means to be gifted that causes them to exclude many children who are actually gifted. However, other teachers have the ability to see a student's potential, even if they are not able to identify them as gifted. Teachers tend to think that students who are high performing, attentive, and well behaved are the most likely to be gifted. In actuality, while some of these students may be gifted, these are more likely to be characteristics of bright students who are properly placed in an appropriate academic setting. Teachers often overlook students who may be bored, hyperactive, or unmotivated. While these can be characteristics of problem students, these are also often characteristics of students who are gifted but not in an appropriate academic setting. Many gifted students who do not feel challenged simply fail to perform at tasks they have already achieved mastery at or are bored by. Some teachers participating in questionnaires done by gifted organizations state that students should "earn" the right to be in a gifted program by performing well in their regular classroom setting. This causes many gifted students to be overlooked.

Parents should feel confident in taking responsibility for their child's identification, and not be swayed by a teacher's estimation of their child. Parents have the right and authority to have their child tested independently based on their own intuitions about their child.

CHAPTER 2

Two Kinds of Giftedness

Once a child is identified as gifted, it is very helpful to have as much information as possible in order to parent her best. It is helpful to know that all children typically fall into one of two categories: concrete-sequential and abstract-spatial. Understanding what category your child is a part of can help you parent her better, place appropriate expectations on her, and know how to address her specific strengths and weaknesses.

Concrete-Sequential

Concrete-sequential children are the typical children people think of with regard to gifted children. Typically, when referring to gifted children, concrete-sequential, or auditory learners, are the most easily identifiable and stereotyped. They are very orderly—not a paper out of place in their desk or a lost homework assignment.

A concrete-sequential child will prefer to learn through written and spoken words. Not surprisingly, concrete-sequential children do well in school because most teachers are concrete-sequential learners and teach in a way that makes sense to children who are also concrete-sequential learners.

Concrete-sequential learners are often referred to as auditory learners. They do exceptionally well at processing information that they hear. These students prefer a quiet learning environment with a specific learning space. They also have a knack for remembering text that they read. A concrete-sequential learner likes specific directions, rules, and a schedule. Concrete-sequential learners want the "right" way to do things, and want them done that way exclusively.

A concrete sequential student struggles with working with a partner or cooperatively. This student might have a harder time taking risks or trying new things. They have a difficult time when things change, and get frustrated with people who do not follow the rules. Exceptions do not exist for concrete-sequential children.

Abstract-Spatial

On the opposite side of the spectrum are abstract-spatial learners. Abstract-spatial students are a little bit harder for people to accept as gifted because they are so different from what most people consider gifted. Their desks and bedrooms are often messy to the onlooker, while making sense to them. An abstract-spatial student loves surprises, working on many tasks at the same time, and having lots of room to be creative in how he completes tasks and solves problems. Additionally, they love any type of creative or open-ended assignment that allows for free thinking. They need pictures, graphs, and diagrams to learn. They may need to have information repeated to them several times because they do not have the auditory skills of concrete-sequential learners. These students work well in bustling environments where they can talk and discuss. Cooperative work is exciting and inspiring to them. They thrive on praise and on relationships as a part of learning.

Abstract-spatial students have a difficult time working in a quiet environment. Repetitive tasks and memorization are not successful learning strategies for their personalities. They do not like being told there is only one right answer, or being limited to a specific strategy for solving a problem. Being given only one task or not being given enough time are also difficult situations for an abstract-spatial learner to be placed in. Not surprisingly, most abstract-spatial students do not like school because there is often little room in the traditional classroom for their creativity and free spiritedness.

 Alert

Parents who have children who are abstract-spatial should be on guard against prejudices in the school system, and even by themselves. Even in their own homes, abstract-spatial students are so different from concrete-sequential students that people are reticent to test them for a gifted program. Parents can help by pursuing outside testing, particularly if the parents are gifted or have other children previously identified as gifted.

Identifying Your Child

Parents who know what to look for can easily determine whether their child is a concrete-sequential or abstract-spatial learner. Taking a look at the following checklist will help you identify your child.

Signs of a Concrete-Sequential Learner

Following are many of the qualities commonly seen in concrete-sequential learners. Your child may have some of these qualities as well as a few of those from the abstract-spatial checklist. You are looking for types of qualities which most align with your child's personality.

✓ Bedroom is orderly
✓ Remembers important dates
✓ Prefers reading and listening over symbols and images
✓ Likes lists and specific directions
✓ Focuses well on a single task

✓ Needs a learning environment that is structured and scheduled

✓ Prefers straightforward discussion

Signs of an Abstract-Spatial Learner

While this checklist is by no means exhaustive, it gives parents a quick look at some of the behavioral characteristics that a child who is abstract-spatial might display. Most abstract-spatial children demonstrate many of these qualities, but will not necessarily have all of them.

✓ Bedroom is messy

✓ Forgets about homework or important due dates

✓ Prefers symbols and images

✓ Frequently loses things

✓ Likes being given a specific task with the freedom to complete it in his own way and time frame

✓ Is usually in the middle of several projects

✓ Needs a learning environment with flexibility and freedom

✓ Jokes and makes friends easily

🔔 Alert

Parents of students who are abstract-spatial need to be aware of a few concerns. People are often quick to label an abstract-spatial child as lazy, distracted, or even as having a learning disability. The most common misdiagnosis for a gifted child who is abstract-spatial is Attention Deficit Disorder. Parents should be very careful before allowing any additional label to be placed on a child who is simply demonstrating the characteristics of giftedness.

Other Combinations

Concrete-sequential and abstract-spatial are the most frequently seen types of giftedness. However, children can also be categorized as concrete-spatial or abstract-sequential, both of which are less common.

 **Question**

How should knowing whether my child is a concrete-sequential or abstract-spatial learner affect my parenting?
Parents need to remember that there is no one-size-fits-all style for parenting. This is especially true for parents who have multiple children. It is important to make sure that your parenting is tailored to your child. One child may need a chore chart with pictures and boxes to check while another needs a list with words to cross off. Just like in the classroom, children need equal opportunity to be successful, which does not necessarily mean completely identical parenting.

The Effect of Birth Order

One of the interesting phenomena with regard to concrete-sequential and abstract-spatial learners is in regard to birth order. First-born children and only children are likely to be concrete-sequential learners, while second-born children are likely to be auditory-spatial children. It is important to be cautious if you have two children. Many parents find it easy to believe that their first-born child is gifted because they demonstrate so many of the characteristics that people commonly associate with giftedness. However, students that are abstract-spatial are just as gifted, but in a less easily accepted manner. Parents of abstract-sequential children might even go so far as to say that their abstract-spatial child is not actually gifted because the stereotypes on what giftedness is are so ingrained in society. Children after the first born and second born are likely to be a combination of the two in lesser degrees of intensity.

 Fact

Interestingly, most gifted children grow up to marry a gifted person of the opposite type than their own. Concrete-sequential learners tend to marry abstract-spatial individuals and vice versa. Perhaps people are drawn to a person who fills in the gaps where their skills are lacking.

What to Do Once You Know

The most important thing for parents to remember, once again, is that being able to identify your child as concrete-sequential or abstract-spatial is not meant to be a cure-all for your child. Understanding learning styles just gives a clearer, fuller picture of who your child is and how they think. It is an extension of the explanation giftedness provides, but it should never be an excuse. Knowing your child is one type of learner or the other should not exempt them from the goals and responsibilities of the family. Instead, this knowledge should help you frame expectations in keeping with your child's abilities as well as help you know how to communicate effectively with your unique child.

Oftentimes, parents are dismayed to have a child of a different learning style than their own. It can be difficult for parents to understand how their child is learning and processing information. This is particularly true when both parents are concrete-sequential and their child is abstract-spatial. Parents need to remember that their child can no more change their learning style than change their hair color. Learning style is a part of a child's fundamental makeup, much like eye color or height. Knowing whether a child is a concrete-sequential or abstract-spatial learner can help parents see their child more fully, but a parent should use that knowledge to strengthen their bonds with their child as opposed to trying to change her. Neither learning style is inherently better than the other, although concrete-sequential children seem to have an easier time adapting to and blending into society. Help your child know how to become successful while remaining true to herself. Too many children feel the need to conform to the mandates of society at the expense of their individuality. Make sure that you are a positive voice for your child and not just another loud voice trying to get her to be just like everyone else.

When Your Children Have Different Learning Styles

Many parents wonder what to do when one child is an abstract-spatial and another is a concrete-sequential. Parents are unsure how to parent each child as an individual without facing the protests of, "That's not fair!" Parents can help children who are very different by making sure not to value one child's learning style over another. Remind your children that they both have strengths that are valuable to the family's success as a whole as well as areas where they need to work harder. It is easy to praise the concrete-sequential child because their skills are so much easier to apply to the family. Parents can avoid this by assigning chores and tasks that support their child's skills. Remember that equality can be achieved in a variety of ways. A concrete-sequential child may like setting the table, putting away dishes, remembering to take the trash out on a specific day; an abstract-spatial child may like helping plan the dinner menu, taking the dog for a walk, or working in the garden. Additionally, a concrete-spatial child may like to have a specific chore schedule while an abstract-spatial child may like a window of time within which to complete their assigned tasks. Everyone can have the same number of chores without completing the same chores.

 **Essential**

Some families have found a chore strategy that works really well if they have a variety of learning styles. Parents make a list of chores, along with regularity and completion times (e.g., unload the dishwasher each morning, vacuum the living room on Tuesdays and Saturdays, or dust the family room weekly). Children then sign up for a certain number of chores each week. No one feels as though this is unfair because they are all completing the same number of chores.

Strategies to Help the Abstract-Spatial Learner

Abstract-spatial learners need their parents to provide aid in their weaker areas as well as support and encouragement regarding their strengths. Parents can help their child complete tasks by taking pictures, posting schedules, or drawing small symbols to acknowledge their visual nature. It is helpful for parents to make sure their child is looking them directly in the eyes when giving directives. They may find having their child repeat back the directions helps as well. While abstract-spatial learners do not like to make lists themselves, they are sometimes helpful as a point of reference for the child. Abstract-spatial children can benefit from a flexible schedule that provides room for individual exploration as well as freedom. Warning your child five to ten minutes before they will be expected to complete a task allows them to get to a stopping point despite their singular focus. Abstract-spatial students also benefit greatly from an alternative school environment where their skills and talents are celebrated.

Looking to the Future

Abstract-Spatial students are typically very good at looking at the big picture. They are also highly creative and individual thinkers who find new ways to solve problems. They experience great success at careers that utilize these skills. Parents can introduce their child to fields in engineering, computer programming, or architecture, for example. Some other careers where they find great success include counseling, photography and other creative arts, as well as physics and experimental sciences.

Strategies to Help the Concrete-Sequential Learner

Concrete-sequential children typically do very well in most environments, however it is important to remember that they need help in their areas of weakness as well. To help your child be more successful at completing tasks, make sure you speak to them instead of leaving a list since most concrete-sequential students process information well auditorily, especially boys. Concrete-sequential kids can benefit from learning how to be flexible and build resiliency since change and unexpected events can derail their efforts. Parents can help with these skills by occasionally having spontaneous activities or changing routines. They can also teach their child that it is okay to get a little messy, let their hair down, and not take life so seriously all the time. Concrete-sequential children benefit from learning to adapt to other people as well. Your concrete-sequential child needs to learn that there are other ways to do things, and that their way is not always the best. Look for opportunities to help them see how a different perspective might add meaning as well as how alternate viewpoints can be equally valid. Hosting debates or playing the Devil's advocate can challenge your concrete-sequential child.

Looking to the Future

Concrete-Sequential students are very organized and love patterns. They thrive in environments that value structure and organization. Any profession that uses lists, computer generated tasks and formulas, and automated processes are great for a concrete-sequential child.

Parents can show their children examples of successful concrete-sequential adults who are lawyers, teachers, or doctors. Some concrete-sequential learners may also become writers, statisticians, financial analysts, or project managers in a variety of fields based on their individual interests.

Parents can find great comfort in learning this exciting information about their unique and wonderful child. Finding out whether a child is abstract-spatial or concrete-sequential is like adding a missing piece to a complicated jigsaw puzzle. It is a piece of a complicated jigsaw puzzle that helps make the picture just a little bit clearer, but possibly still not quite yet complete.

CHAPTER 3

Common Misconceptions about Gifted Children

The word "gifted" stirs up many thoughts and feelings in those who hear it. Sadly, there are many misconceptions about what being gifted truly means. Our culture's common myths about giftedness can be dispelled by an examination of accurate data on giftedness. Information can help teachers, parents, and gifted students themselves become a voice for change with regard to perceptions on being gifted.

Gifts Versus Gifted

An important distinction must be made in terminology regarding understanding giftedness. No one can dispute that all children are very special and each have their own unique gifts. However, for the purposes of this book and to help the parents of the gifted receive the most specific, accurate information, the term gifted has a specific meaning. Gifted in this context refers to students who have been tested and determined to be in the top 95th percentile of intelligence compared to their age-level peers. This can also refer to students with an IQ tested at over 130. It is helpful to understand this information when confronted with the idea that all children are gifted. Again, all children have wonderful talents and gifts, but the term "gifted" means something distinct and quantifiable.

Gardner's Multiple Intelligences

Many parents searching for information on raising a gifted child stumble onto the work of Howard Gardner. Gardner is famous for pioneering the idea of multiple intelligences in the education field. His theory states that there are seven different types of intelligence:

- Linguistic
- Logical-mathematical
- Musical
- Bodily-kinesthetic
- Spatial
- Interpersonal
- Intrapersonal

These intelligences are often referred to as areas of giftedness; however, the more traditional scholars in gifted education adhere to the three primary, testable areas of giftedness. These are verbal, quantitative, and spatial.

Gardner's intelligences are helpful in the education community in making sure that students are taught concepts through a variety of means in order to address all students' learning styles, but should not be confused with the actual definition of giftedness.

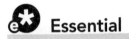 **Essential**

For parents wanting to investigate Howard Gardner's theories more, an excellent resource is *You're Smarter than You Think: A Kid's Guide to Multiple Intelligences*, by Thomas Armstrong. Parents and students can take the quiz in this book to learn more about their areas of intelligence as well as helpful strategies for optimum learning environments based on their intelligences.

Why the Labels?

Parents may be wondering why we have these labels of gifted, profoundly gifted, or high IQ. Are they necessary? They seem to make things more complicated. This is a common question both within and outside of the gifted community. Friends and family members may feel confused and uncertain when presented with the information that a child is gifted. Some may think using the term gifted seems elitist or prideful.

Unfortunately, the term gifted has been misused throughout the education community, which adds to the confusion surrounding giftedness. Many educators are also not trained to identify the gifted, and thus inaccurately tell parents that their child is gifted. Educators joke that all parents think their children are gifted. However, in technical terms, "gifted" actually consists of a definition, tests, and services for students within this special needs population.

The label of gifted should be a distinction for students who have been properly identified and are hopefully receiving services and programs to meet their needs. A student who is appropriately termed gifted has tested in the 95th percentile on a recognized cognitive abilities test. Students who are known to be gifted are a special population within the larger population. Gifted students think and behave differently from the other children in that larger population. As such, they require special distinction and services for their different needs.

No one would balk at a student being identified as dyslexic or autistic and receiving services for those special needs. For some reason, the term "gifted" makes people feel uncomfortable, but it serves an important purpose as part of the identification process. Perhaps in the future, a less controversial term can be agreed upon; however, for right now, the term gifted is most commonly recognized.

Is "Gifted" a Dirty Word?

Many parents prefer to use terms such as "bright," "intelligent," or "overachiever," because of the common negative implication with the term gifted. Parents are often afraid to say that their child is gifted for fear of the reaction, even within a school or educational setting.

Question

What should you do in a school setting where the educators and administrators seem misinformed about giftedness?
Keep in mind that most educators and administrators receive little or no training in identifying and making accommodations for gifted students. Therefore, parents can help by providing current books, articles, and research to school professionals. Additionally, offering to help by starting a parent's group, leading after-school enrichment groups, or volunteering in the classroom can be beneficial. Let the school personnel know that you want to work with them, not against them, to create the best possible learning environment for all of the children there.

Instead of shying away from the term gifted, parents can help educate people on what it really means to be gifted. Advocating and providing accurate information on how gifted students are identified, how they think and act differently, and why they need services will go a long way in helping others understand giftedness.

Who Does This to Their Kids?

A common myth exists that giftedness is something parents have "done" to their children. Other parents and family members may feel that parents of gifted students somehow pushed them to be this way through flashcards, enrichment programs, or coaching. Some gifted parents do utilize these strategies to help their children learn, as do many parents of students who are not gifted. However, these strategies do not make a child gifted. Giftedness is an alternate way of thinking that children are born with, and no amount of drilling can change that.

Often, parents are faced with criticism for choosing to test their child or to enroll their child in services for the gifted. Many parents feel that all children are best served by a standard curriculum. Some schools even market themselves this way, by telling parents that all children will receive exactly the same curriculum in a grade level regardless of the teacher. While this can initially sound like a good thing, it is not a good fit for a gifted child.

If a gifted child is not challenged on a daily, sometimes hourly, basis, they will fail to thrive. Gifted students who are not given appropriate curriculum for their needs will wither like flowers that are not given water or sunlight. In an attempt to find mental stimulation of any kind, they will often act out, distract other students, or simply give up. In their effort to please their teacher, some gifted children will even pretend not to know the curriculum being taught—sometimes even fooling themselves into learning the same knowledge over and over, year after year.

A traditional curriculum fits most children most of the time, which is why schools teach this way. Again, for most students, this is perfectly acceptable and adequately challenging. Students who are in the top and bottom 5 percent of the population need something more, though. Most people are not upset when students in the bottom 5 percent receive services for their special needs. It would be cruel to expect them to work in the same way as other students when they have been identified as having special needs.

Gifted students are in exactly the same position, but on the opposite side of the spectrum. Again, it should seem cruel to expect them to do the same work as other students when they have been identified as having special needs. To expect them, day after day, to perform tasks they have already mastered and find little challenge in, is a punishment with grievous consequences.

Why Can't the Teacher Just Do Grouping?

Often, parents and opponents of gifted education propose grouping as a possible accommodation for gifted students. There are several types of groups/grouping, some of which have had a certain level of success for gifted students.

Cooperative Learning

Cooperative learning is when students work together in groups to complete a task. This is most commonly seen in traditional classrooms. Teachers typically try to place students of various abilities together to complete a task. The theory behind this type of grouping is that the students work together to combine their various strengths and weaknesses, therefore accommodating each other while completing the task. The reality is that the gifted students often "tutor" the lower-ability students and the middle-ability students are lost in the shuffle. However, when students are grouped by achievement first, then placed into cooperative groups to complete a task, all the students perform better.

Ability Grouping

Ability grouping is the practice of grouping students of like ability levels together for core subjects or specific tasks. Studies have shown that this type of grouping is highly beneficial for students at all levels, but particularly for gifted students. Gifted students are provided instruction at the level they need, and are able to work with students of similar skill levels.

Ability grouping is very common in elementary school, particularly for reading. As children get older, and their proficiencies become more disparate, ability grouping is utilized less frequently. The plain and simple fact is that teachers are not trained to handle ability grouping in terms of instruction and classroom management. Teachers do not have the time or resources necessary to continue ability grouping, which even at lower levels is a strain. Many teachers are also resistant to ability grouping because they enjoy a particular curriculum and don't want to vary it for different abilities of students. Furthermore, if all students are allowed to learn at their own rate, it is hard to predict what levels incoming students will be at for the following year. This makes it hard for teachers to plan what they are going to teach, and the school will generally only provide one grade level of curriculum. Unfortunately, the system is simply not set up to accommodate ability grouping.

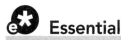 **Essential**

Parents can advocate for ability grouping at the classroom, school, and district level. They can be a powerful voice requesting change to help all students. Parents can also help by offering to volunteer in the classroom. In the early years, parents are usually active and involved in the classrooms of their children. However, volunteerism typically thins out in the upper elementary years and beyond, when it is most necessary due to the greater range between students' abilities.

Additionally, many parents protest ability grouping, in part because they feel it limits students, and in part because they do not like it when their child is not in the highest ability-level group. Parents fail to recognize that when students are taught at their own level, regardless of what level that is, everyone learns and achieves more. Some also feel like once a child is put in a lower track, they get a lesser education (worse teachers, not as much pushing for achievement, exposure to other lower-level kids, so less challenge), so they are locked in and can never break out to a higher level. Parents and educators must work together to find a solution where the individual needs of each student are met.

Why Aren't Gifted Kids Good at Everything?

One of the most commonly held myths about gifted students is that they are good at everything. This is very rarely the case. While gifted students do have high IQs and are keen learners, they are not good at everything. Gifted students are tested in three primary areas: quantitative, verbal, and nonverbal skills. They typically will be primarily gifted in one skill area. Sometimes a student will be gifted in two areas. Very rarely will a student be gifted in all three areas.

Students who are gifted quantitatively are very good at mathematics as well as logical reasoning tasks. However, that does not mean that they are gifted in verbal areas. In the same way, students with superior language skills may be weaker in mathematics. This can be true for any child who has a particular academic strength in any area. It does not mean they are suddenly good at every academic learning skill. Some schools allow students to participate in their gifted program if they are gifted in only one area, feeling that students can rise to the additional challenge in the other areas. This can be successful, particularly if students have a learning disability or did not perform well on testing day, causing their true potential to go undocumented. Many students thrive in an environment of high expectations.

Schools handle giftedness in different ways. Some schools have students receive additional support services in the classroom for their area of giftedness while others pull students out of the classroom to receive separate services in their area. Other schools let students participate in pull-out enrichment programs that may or may not address their area of giftedness, but will provide stimulation to keep the student from boredom. Still other schools have self-contained classrooms for students who test high enough in one area or a combination of areas. Occasionally, a school will allow a student to go to another classroom in a higher grade level for instruction in their area of giftedness. The size and style of school programs are dependent on the number of gifted students identified in a grade and school, the training of individual teachers, and the budgets of the school district, among other constraints.

So You Think You're Better Than Me Now?

One of the common cries against giftedness is the suspected tendency for elitism. People often oppose gifted programs for fear that students and parents will begin to think that their children are somehow better than other children.

This fear is mostly unwarranted. Sadly, there are some parents of gifted students who bring truth to this stereotype. However, the same can be said for parents whose children have not been identified as gifted. The propensity for overestimating a child can overtake any parent, regardless of what their special ability is. The best antidote is one mentioned previously in this chapter: education. The more that people know about giftedness, the less likely they are to have false assumptions about raising gifted children.

Most parents of gifted children are easy to spot. They are the overwhelmed, confused, and frustrated parents pulling their hair out trying to meet the complex needs of their little whirlwind. They are the parents who are seeking help, promising that they didn't do this to their child! They are the last ones to say their child is better than yours. In fact, most probably wish they were not faced with the challenges and complexities of raising a gifted child.

CHAPTER 4

Development in Gifted Children

When trying to understand the difference between gifted and nongifted students, it helps to look at how giftedness can affect traditional child development. There are several significant differences that help explain many of the difficulties students feel in various settings. This information will also help parents better help their child reach their full potential by holding reasonable and appropriate expectations based on their child's strengths and areas for growth.

Asynchronous Development

The term "asynchronous development" commonly refers to two different phenomena in giftedness. Perhaps more than any other knowledge, an understanding of asynchronous development can help parents encourage, motivate, and challenge their gifted child. Asynchronous, by definition, means "not at the same rate." When this is applied to child development, it means that the child's rate of development is not the same as that of other age-level peers.

In the gifted community, asynchronous development has two separate meanings. Primarily, asynchronous development is used to reference students whose cognitive growth in one area is at such an accelerated rate that other areas of development are lacking. They may be very good at mathematics, but one grade level or below in reading.

Additionally, asynchronous development can refer to a child's physical development being out of sync with their cognitive development. This can mean that parents see their child's large vocabulary and advanced reasoning, but are frustrated when they demonstrate age-appropriate responses to circumstances in their lives.

Asynchronous Development in Physical Development

Most gifted students experience some degree of asynchronous development in their physical development. Often, the higher the level of giftedness, the more asynchronous the development. Gifted children, particularly profoundly gifted children, are often very skewed in their development. Parents may notice that their children may know their times tables, but are unable to jump rope. Another example is children who are reading at age three, but can't swing themselves. Asynchronous development explains why gross- and fine-motor skills are often delayed for gifted students. The brain establishes a hierarchy, with physical tasks ranking at the bottom of its cognitive priority list.

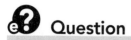 Question

How can you help your child when you notice asynchronous development?
For most children, simply discussing their difficulty can help ease the emotional burden. For example, many gifted kindergarteners have difficulty with handwriting. Explaining to them that their brain is working very hard at math and reading and has less energy for handwriting makes sense. Gifted students are logical above all else. Any time you can provide her with a reasonable explanation for why her brain and body are functioning in a certain way will help her.

Asynchronous Development in Cognitive Skills

Another area of asynchronous development deals with a student's particular areas of giftedness. Students are commonly tested on verbal, quantitative, and nonverbal intelligences. Asynchronous development in the cognitive realm refers to students being highly gifted in one of these areas while being "normal" in the other areas, or not as highly gifted. Many feel that the more skilled a student is in one area, the greater his deficit may be in another area. This is evidenced in students who are highly gifted in mathematics, but have a learning disability in language arts.

 Alert

> Many educators are unaware of the phenomena of asynchronous development, especially in the cognitive realm. When told that a student is gifted, they may assume that a student is gifted in all three areas. This is very rarely the case. Sometimes students will be highly gifted in two areas. More often, a student is highly gifted in one area and either bright or average in the other areas. Parents can advocate for their child by letting the teacher know their child's areas of giftedness. That way, teachers (and parents) can properly challenge a child in his area of giftedness while maintaining appropriate expectations in the areas where he is not gifted.

Twice Exceptional

The most profound cases of asynchronous development can qualify as being twice exceptional. "Twice exceptional" is a term applied to many gifted kids who are gifted in one area but severely lagging in another area, to the point of qualifying as having a learning disability. Most commonly, students who are very gifted in quantitative skills also have dyslexia or dysgraphia—the two most common language disorders currently diagnosed. The term twice exceptional is also applied to a student who has been identified as gifted but also has a behavioral or psychological disorder such as ADHD or who is bipolar.

Skewed Skills

Understanding that students can have asynchronous development helps parents accept their child's skewed skills. For example, a parent may be frustrated that his child can do complex mathematical computations but cannot tie her shoes. This is a perfect example of the skewed skills for a gifted child. Parents can help their children by supporting them in their areas of strength while providing the necessary assistance in the areas where they are slower at learning. This is a great opportunity for parents to gain humility. Their child may be exceptional in academics, but as they struggle through some of the delayed motor and social skills, parents can begin to understand the struggles other parents go through.

Areas of Delay

As knowledge of asynchronous development grows, parents want to know what to expect from their child. It is important to note that all children, gifted children included, are individuals. The rate of any child's growth is variable and it is best not to hold a child to a certain schedule or chart unless a parent is prepared to set herself up for disappointment. However, in general, the three areas where gifted children can be delayed are gross-motor skills, fine-motor skills, and social skills. Gross-motor skills can include delays in walking, running, playing sports, and other large-motion skills. Fine-motor skill delays may affect students' ability to write (especially proper pencil grip and precise handwriting), tie their shoes, learn to jump rope, and participate in sports. Social-skill delays may include baby talking into early elementary school, maintaining imaginary friends through the early school years, difficulty playing with other students, and delays in developing boy-girl relationships.

Areas of Early Development

While there are many areas where gifted children might be delayed, there are also many areas where gifted children can develop earlier than their age-level peers. The specific areas where they develop early are usually indicative of where their strongest cognitive area of giftedness lies. Many gifted students begin to talk at a very early age. They also begin to use verbal skills to negotiate deals or debate with their parents at a very young age. As a parent, choose which battles are most important to the harmony and success of the family, and learn to compromise on other less important areas.

Remember though, while your child may be learning early debating and discussion, you are the parent and the authority. Their giftedness is not an excuse for them to argue, disobey, or defy you. It is merely an explanation for why they are behaving in a certain way.

 **Essential**

From a young age, it is important to teach your gifted child the appropriate way to hold discussions as well as express differing opinions. Many gifted students have difficulty expressing their thoughts and opinions with the appropriate tone and volume for civilized debates. You can help by hosting dinner-time debates over neutral topics to allow opportunities to develop these skills. This will teach your child how to discuss concerns without appearing overly aggressive or volatile with teachers and peers.

Young gifted students can also demonstrate early aptitude for spatial tasks by building complex structures with puzzles, building toys, or grasping early geometric concepts. These skills can be fun for the whole family, as parents encourage the use of a variety of materials.

Students can also demonstrate early aptitude for logical or mathematical skills. These are shown through the unending questions of how things work, why the world operates in a specific way, and a curiosity with numbers, money, and other mathematical calculations. Parents can encourage these skills primarily by answering questions and investing in a child's interests. It can be difficult to have the patience to address the seemingly endless questions a two to three year old has, but it is important for parents to take the time to answer their child's questions clearly and with detail. Gifted children know when they are given a lazy answer, and too many will squelch a child's curiosity as well as her trust in you as a resource for her cognitive development.

 **Question**

How can I encourage my child's interests when she is driving me crazy with all the questions? I just don't have all the answers!
Many parents of gifted children feel this way. Frankly, gifted children are exhausting with their intensity and single-mindedness. Anyone would begin to feel overwhelmed, and a parent cannot possibly know the answers to their endless questions. In these instances, it is perfectly acceptable to say, "I don't know the answer, but how about if we find out together?" Follow up with a trip to the library, a research session on the Internet, or a visit to a local museum. Teaching a child where to find the answer to his question is far more valuable than simply providing an answer—and infinitely better than making up an answer!

How Development Affects Relationships

Gifted children may also demonstrate delays in their social and emotional growth as a part of their asynchronous development. This can be particularly frustrating and confusing to parents of gifted students. Often, this is the result of the child's high intelligence giving a false sense of maturity to the outside world. One moment a parent can be discussing physics of motion with their child and the next trying to teach him not to take a toy without asking. A child who knows all his multiplication tables may still be afraid of the dark. The answer lies with how the gifted brain learns and processes information. A gifted brain processes information based on hierarchy. Gifted students will typically have tremendous difficulty reading social cues. Their brain simply does not allot many resources to the social and emotional arenas.

❗ Alert

A parent can help her child become better at understanding social cues by providing a concrete rule to follow. Gifted children are logical at heart, and a clear explanation is always the best. Saying, "When you raise your hand more than once during a speaker's presentation, it makes the other students think you are hogging the spotlight and is also selfish because they do not get a turn. Only raise your hand to answer one question during a presentation, unless no one else raises their hand." While it may seem harsh, a gifted child will value the clear feedback without taking offense. It is also helpful to practice these behaviors when you know your child might be facing them, such as before a play date or field trip.

Why They Are so Good with Adults

Gifted children tend to gravitate toward adults or older children. They instinctively seek out older individuals who are receptacles of knowledge ripe for questioning. Adults are also less likely to take offense at social blunders, perhaps even finding them humorous. Very lucky gifted children will find those who share their interests, look past their age, and treat them respectfully like equals. While a child may be young chronologically, they are mature in their interests and conversational skills when regarding a topic of interest to them.

Why They Are Bad with Peers

The very skills that make gifted children good with adults make their relationships with their classmates difficult. The topics they are interested in are simply not of interest to their age-level friends. They tend to make up complicated games with even more complex rules. Add to that their inability to judge the reactions and social cues given by other students, and parents are left with very lonely children.

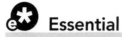 **Essential**

Parents can help their child by teaching him what to look for in conversations. Practicing pretend scenarios can teach a child to recognize cues from the other person and learn to interpret them. Teach your child to take turns speaking, allowing the other person a turn for every two to three sentences he speaks. Practice asking questions to draw the other person into conversation. Some areas to demonstrate when someone is not interested include the listener looking away, trying to extract himself from the conversation, and interrupting.

Many parents find the early acquisition of skills for their child exhilarating, while the delays can be terribly frustrating. The extremes are particularly difficult. While there is no finite timetable for when a child levels out in her development, it is helpful to remember that the majority of all children become functioning members of society despite areas where their skills are lagging. They still manage to have full and exciting lives, so parents should try not to worry too much about their child's development and focus on loving and encouraging him in all areas.

CHAPTER 5

How Gifted Children Feel

C hildren who are identified as gifted experience a wide range of emotions. This chapter will examine the unique emotions many gifted children feel, not all of them as wonderful as one might think. Discussing the emotions gifted children are experiencing will help their parents better understand and aid them. Many parents are unaware of the variety of emotions that gifted children experience. Some parents also feel unprepared to handle the intensity of emotions that gifted children feel. These facets of emotional experience can bewilder parents, leaving them searching for answers.

Pride

Many children feel a sense of pride, much like that of their parents, upon hearing that they are gifted. While most of these students do not understand exactly what it means to be gifted, they can usually determine that it is a very good thing. Parents usually present the news with joy and excitement, which children pick up on. Older children, with some understanding of what it means to be gifted, may also be very proud of themselves for achieving this type of status.

ⓔ Question

Are you helping your child feel positive about being gifted?
If you want to help your child, make sure to remember that being gifted explains something about her, but it does not define her. You should encourage your child to reach her full potential, but make sure you are not causing her to feel too much pressure or that how you feel about her is contingent upon her performance. Giftedness is about how your child thinks, not who she is as a person.

It is important that your child knows that being gifted says something positive about his abilities, and he should absolutely be proud of himself for all his achievements, but being gifted does not make him better or superior to his peers, colleagues, and friends at school, nor does it give him preferential treatment at home or in outside activities. Using his gifted status to gain special privileges or be condescending to his classmates is not only unkind but can lead to further irresponsible behavior and a poor attitude in the future. Teaching your child about healthy pride versus conceit is a great lesson that can help him successfully navigate his school years and times with his friends.

This is much more difficult than it might appear at first glance. Many, many gifted children struggle with feeling an inflated sense of self. They can become arrogant and boastful. This causes difficulty with teachers as well as peers. If parents know that this is a particular struggle with their child, they may even consider not telling their child about their test scores or that they are gifted. The primary reason to discuss their child's giftedness and abilities is if it will be of benefit to the child. For some children the knowledge is too much for them, especially at a young age.

It is important for a gifted child to be reminded that his giftedness explains the way that he thinks. His brain thinks in a different way from other children, but it is not necessarily better. Many gifted children benefit from volunteer work with special needs children.

This can serve as a good reminder that each person's brain functions differently. His intelligence is one facet of who he is, but there is also much more to him than that, in the same way that a special needs student is more than just his special needs.

 Alert

One area where parents may have to make a hard choice is contests. There are many different programs gifted children can become involved in that give awards at the end. For some children, participating in these activities is a great opportunity that allows them to interact with other bright children. For other children, participating in these contests gives them an inflated sense of self and causes them to be arrogant. Each parent needs to evaluate their own child, determine what benefit and harm would occur based on the outcome of the contest, and decide if it is in their child's best interests.

Acceptance

One of the most rewarding emotions that students feel upon hearing that they are gifted is that of acceptance. Most gifted children recognize from a very early age that they are innately different from other kids. They know that they do not connect with their age-level peers, and that something is just a little off in their interactions. When they find out that they are gifted, it might seem as though life finally makes a little more sense.

The feeling of acceptance is especially true for students who are promptly placed in a program at school or in their community where they are interacting with other gifted students, perhaps for the first time. These children in particular will feel the sense of acceptance. Many students describe it as "finally belonging."

This may be a different experience for homeschooled gifted children. Children who are homeschooled may be insulated from the fear of not being accepted that other gifted children experience because they are not comparing themselves to other children. Still, gifted children who are homeschooled may enjoy being a part of programs and groups that allow them to interact with other gifted children for the sake of building relationships and learning teamwork.

Loneliness

While many students feel a sense of belonging, sometimes giftedness can also have the opposite effect. Some children describe a sense of loneliness. Although finding out she is gifted is a good thing, a child may only see that she is somehow different and set apart from other students (usually at an age when being different is the last thing they want to be!). This can be a result of the way she is treated by parents, teachers, and her peers.

Isolation in School

Loneliness may also be a consequence of programming options in the child's area. If the school district does not provide adequate support, gifted students can be made to feel isolated. She may be the only student doing certain curriculum, which makes her feel ostracized, and eliminates her from social interactions. Additionally, many schools utilize a pull-out program. Often, a student may be the only member of her class or the only student at her school who is participating in the program. This can contribute to the feelings of solitude a gifted student may feel, as she is continually separated from her classmates.

Finally, gifted students learn and behave in ways that are not like other students. This, by its very nature, can cause them to feel set apart from peers. They play more outlandish games, invoke complex rules, desire more in-depth play, and have difficulty sharing. The very characteristics that demonstrate their giftedness create a deep river that may not be easily bridged. All of these factors can create feelings of isolation for a gifted child.

 Alert

Loneliness can usually be addressed and minimized by caring and knowledgeable adults actively involved in a child's life. However, in serious cases, it may lead to depression. If your child is feeling an overwhelming sense of loneliness, you may want to seek professional assistance. Warning signs include retreating from loved ones, refusal to participate in previously enjoyed activities, excessive emotional outbursts of tears or anger, atypical lethargy, and dramatic changes in eating habits.

Judgment

After your child has been identified as gifted, he can begin to feel as though he is being judged. Students may think that now their parents and teachers expect more of them.

These feelings may be legitimate. Teachers of gifted students can often place undue burdens on them. They may expect perfection in studies or behavior from students who have been identified as gifted, and feel judged based on their performance in these areas. Remember that not all educators have received training in how to handle gifted students. You can help by acting as an advocate for your child within their school and classroom. Provide teachers with helpful articles or books (such as those in the appendix) so that they have a good understanding of what it means to be gifted as well as reasonable expectations for your gifted child.

Judgment from Parents

Gifted children can also feel judged by their parents. Many express feeling as though they are disappointing their parents or letting them down. Children fear that their parents may love them less if they get a poor grade on a test or if they are not good at something right away. Gifted kids often hear their parents discussing their skills or bragging about them to their peers. This leads them to feel as though their parents are only seeing their intelligence and not the other aspects of their personality.

There are steps you can take to help your child avoid these feelings of judgment. Parents can start by understanding that giftedness is just part of your child. It helps explain who your child is, how he thinks and learns, but it does not define him. Make sure to tell your child about a variety of different areas where he has strengths and weaknesses. Share with him qualities you admire unrelated to his academic abilities like his perseverance in baseball, his kindness to his little sister, or the way he always takes out the trash when he is asked to. Just as parents are more diverse than their jobs, children are more diverse than their school experiences.

Remember, also, that giftedness is determined by how your child's brain works. It does not mean that he will be good at everything, or that everything comes easily to him. Demonstrating acceptance of who he is will remove some of the sense of judgment he may be experiencing.

Alert

One tip for building a healthy self-image in your gifted child is to encourage her to try new activities. It might even be helpful to have her try a sport or activity that she is not particularly good at. Be aware that she may try to quit if she does not think she is skilled right away. Make sure you encourage her efforts at this activity as opposed to just her performance. Gifted students benefit greatly from seeing that they can find enjoyment in activities without having to be the best. This also builds perseverance when she continues a task that takes practice and effort.

Perfectionism's Early Warning Signs

Parents should also be on guard for signs of perfectionism rooted in these feelings of judgment. Children fear that they will lose their sense of identity or their parents' positive esteem if they fail to perform at a certain level. This can begin at a very young age. What may start out as a healthy determination and drive to succeed can become an obsession with overachieving and being seen as perfect. A parent can address these early warning signs and stave off later perfectionism by praising all of their child's efforts—both successes and failures. Parents can also set an example by making light of their own failures, such as laughing about a missed turn and being bad at directions or the way they have trouble remembering to get everything on the grocery list in one trip. A parent can also never state enough that their love is not conditioned on performance but is unconditional, no matter what they do in school or in life.

 ## Question

When and how is praise most effective for gifted children?
Determining when and how to praise a gifted child can be confusing for a parent. A good rule of thumb is to praise actions that require effort. Gifted children can see through hollow praise, and find it condescending. Also, overly praising actions that did not actually require effort can create a false sense of esteem that makes it even harder for a child to deal with difficult tasks and the failures that are a healthy part of childhood. Your child cannot be good at everything, and it is neglectful to fail to teach them how to handle the challenges that will inevitably come their way in life.

Judgment from Friends and Peers

Gifted students can also feel judged by their peers. Classmates may criticize them because they are always in the highest academic group, break the curve, or because they are often praised by the teacher. If your child is experiencing judgment by peers, remember to tell them that all children are different. Everyone has different strengths in learning as well as areas where they have room for growth. Role playing how to handle these situations may provide resources for your child to draw upon in future situations, especially if they are in elementary school.

Bullying and Jealousy

When your gifted child informs you that she is receiving pushback or judgment from her peers at school as a result of her giftedness, one of the worst things you can do is tell her to ignore it, or ignore it yourself. Gifted children, particularly when a teacher or coach openly praises their achievements, can often incite jealousy from their classmates even if they are the nicest, most humble children around. Unfortunately, this jealousy can grow into targeted bullying. It is wise to talk with your child's teacher, coach, or caregiver if you hear about any kind of open attack or strong criticism placed on your child, and see what you can do to help your child resolve any issues early before they become larger problems.

Fear

Many gifted students express feelings of fear related to their giftedness. This can be for many reasons. Being gifted is, by definition, being different. Children usually fear any type of difference in a society that places a large emphasis on fitting in. Gifted students fear others finding out that they are different. In some schools, being identified as gifted might mean being pulled out of your regular classroom for services or possibly being placed in a self-contained classroom for gifted students. These potential changes can be very frightening for elementary- and even middle school-aged children.

Unique Learners and "Playing Dumb"

Gifted children have struggles coping with the emotions related to being gifted, particularly in a school setting. Students have been known to sabotage their gifted testing for fear of these changes. A gifted child "playing dumb," or purposefully not doing his best in order to avoid change or attention for being different, is a common occurrence. Parents can help their children by explaining from an early age that all students learn differently. Everyone deserves to be challenged at his own individual level, and gifted services are sometimes the best way to challenge a gifted student. Remind them that many students receive those special services from their own classroom teacher, but that there are other teachers who can help them reach their full potential as well. Children who have been taught from a young age to celebrate and value uniqueness seem to have less fear regarding their giftedness.

Fear of Identity Loss and Underachievement

Gifted students can also begin to feel as if their identity is tied to their giftedness. Children who feel this way fear that if they fail to perform to certain standards, they will lose that sense of who they are as a result. Occasionally, students will simply stop trying instead of having to face the possibility of failing. Parents can help their children with these fears by making sure to praise their child's efforts as opposed to their child's inherent abilities. An example would be saying, "I am so proud of how hard you tried on your math test" instead of "You are so smart and good at math!" Make sure to take plenty of time to praise your child for who he is as a special member of your family, not related to his intelligence, in order to build their security, as well.

Confusion

Gifted children are often given a wide variety of responses to their intelligence. Parents may be excited to tell their friends that their child has tested well on an intelligence test on one hand, while on the other hand be irritated that their child asks so many questions.

Teachers may be proud to show off a gifted child in the spelling or geography bee, while also being frustrated with the extra energy and work that a gifted child requires in the classroom. The classroom and school are the sites of the most confusion, as a child struggles to find a way to be challenged while feeling as if that causes a burden to other classmates and an overworked teacher.

⊖! Alert

Children hear everything! Avoid giving your child mixed messages by not talking about them to other adults when they are present. Hearing you brag about them or express disappointment to other adults may send them mixed signals on your expectations for their behavior. It's also a good idea to ask their permission first before sharing stories or anecdotes—especially when they are within earshot. Remember, kids are people, too!

These mixed signals can be confusing to a gifted child. Gifted children already have increased difficulty reading social cues because of the way that their brain works. When adults in their lives send these confusing signals, gifted students can feel as though they need to "turn on" or "turn off" their giftedness to find acceptance from the adults in their lives.

How to Build a Peer Group

One of the best ways to help your child deal with the complex array of emotions she is feeling is by creating a positive and supportive peer group for her. Having friends who understand can give students a place to share their emotions as well as a place to escape from them. Peer groups usually take two forms: in-school groups and outside-school groups.

In-School Peer Groups

Your child has a very small group of peers to reach out to within his classroom. The number is most likely around thirty or fewer based on traditional classroom sizes. You can help your child make friends with his classmates by arranging play dates with other classmates. Try to find out which students have similar interests to make the play date more successful. You can also ask the teacher if there are other students who your child might be more likely to build a bond with. Some teachers may be reluctant to help in this way, but most are receptive to your genuine desire to help your child make friends.

Your child also has other options for peers within his school. Gifted students may find peers with students one to two grades older or younger. They are drawn to younger students because they are often able to serve as a leader or teacher to these younger children. Older students are more likely to have similar interests and relative intelligence. This is nothing to worry about in the elementary school years. Once your child reaches older elementary or middle-school age, it is wise to make sure that peer interactions with older students are supervised or closely monitored because of the more sophisticated influences of older students that your younger child may not be emotionally prepared for.

You can help your child interact with students of varied ages in his school by encouraging involvement in extracurricular activities. Think about having your child join a sewing club or young engineers group. If your school does not have any activities geared toward your child's interests, ask the school officials about the possibility of starting one or volunteer to host one yourself.

 **Question**

Should I be concerned if my children only have one or two friends?
Unlike adults and students who are not gifted, your child may be quite content with only one or two close playmates. Many gifted specialists refer to this close friend as a "safe shelter." As long as your child has at least one playmate, there is no real cause to be concerned. The friends may also change frequently as your child develops new interests and activities, which is also not a cause for alarm.

Outside Peer Groups

Peer groups can be found all throughout the community. While a school has a limited population with limited opportunities for like-minded peers, the community gives a much larger pool to draw from for your child. You can try topic-specific groups if your child has certain interests, like a chess club or a summer program on dinosaurs at your local science museum.

It is important to remember that your child will likely be drawn to students both younger and older than herself. Giftedness is often age blind, as children gravitate to other children with like interests as well as a similar intelligence regardless of their chronological age. Because of her asynchronous development, your ten year old may still love trains, while most children are outgrowing that fascination upon entering school. Support your child and allow her to pursue her interests as long as she desires, while still helping introduce new topics to encourage well roundedness.

CHAPTER 6

How Parents of
the Gifted Feel

There are many helpful resources to assist in dealing with the social and emotional sides of raising gifted children, but very few that deal with the special emotions that come as a parent of a gifted child. Parents of the gifted are under a unique and special strain as they raise these complex youngsters. Most of their parenting peers are offended or surprised when gifted parents attempt to reveal how challenging it is to parent a gifted child. Parents who do not have gifted children think that it must be easy and fun to raise such a bright and precocious child. Gifted parents are left feeling very alone in their emotions and experiences, along with a host of other emotions with which they may be trying to cope.

Lonely

Most gifted parents can recount a particular instance when they realized that they were not like other parents. Whether it was at a parent group, on a play date, or at the playground, a moment came when they realized that they had little in common with the parents of children the same age as their own. Parents of the gifted stop reading parenting magazines when they realize that the information inside just does not fit their child. These can lead to gifted parents feeling a sense of solitude in the already challenging job of parenting.

It stands to reason that if gifted children represent only 5 percent of the population their parents only represent 5 percent of the parent population. While the 95 percent in the majority can find a sense of solidarity, it can be very lonely for the parents in the minority.

Parents of children who are not gifted may not understand how difficult it is to parent a special needs child. They may feel as though the parent of the gifted child is bragging or belittling other children, when the gifted parent is simply trying to find common ground.

There is little comfort to be found unless a gifted parent can locate a particularly understanding group of parents to befriend or find another group of parents whose children are also gifted. The reality is that parents of gifted kids will most likely need to keep searching until they make friends with other parents of gifted kids. It is difficult to imagine having a friend so understanding that they would be interested in hearing a parent of a gifted kid pour out their struggles about how to meet this brilliant kid's needs. They would be perceived as bragging because the other parent just does not understand the complex challenge of raising a gifted child.

Many parents find solace in online gifted parenting groups, where a greater number of parents of gifted children meet together for empathy and support. These can help parents battle the overwhelming feeling of being alone in raising their child.

🄴 Alert

Parents of gifted children may want to exercise particular caution in choosing a pediatrician. Just as educators and other parents may not be familiar with the special needs of gifted children, the same can be true for health care providers. Being with a doctor who does not understand your child's needs can exacerbate their feelings of loneliness. The special needs of gifted children extend even to their physical health. Never stay with a provider who makes you feel foolish, dismisses your concerns, or doesn't allow you to ask questions.

Lack of Understanding

Another common sentiment amongst parents of the gifted is that of a lack of understanding or even judgment. Other parents have trouble fully understanding what it means to raise a gifted child, and have a hard time being sympathetic to the struggles of a gifted parent in raising children who are challenged academically while also meeting their social and emotional needs. Many parents feel as though other parents are judging them in a variety of ways. Some parents sense that other parents or family members think this is something that they have "done" to their children by pushing them too hard or by drilling them from a young age. Whether outsiders are well meaning or mean spirited depends on the occasion, but many feel no reticence in airing their opinions to parents of the gifted.

Concerned family members can be particularly critical. What was good enough for the parent should be good enough for the child, right? After all, the parent turned out just fine. It is helpful to remind family members that there have been considerable advancements in the fields of education and giftedness in the past several decades. There are options available now that were not available then, and it would be foolish not to investigate and take advantage of them.

 Alert

Parents may experience a lack of understanding as they seek resources, as well. For example, parents could be looking for more challenging courses for their child, and ask the teacher if she could suggest things to supplement his classroom learning. Such requests are often met with responses suggesting parents should not push their child but just let him enjoy the learning process. People often see the parents as overachievers pushing their child too hard.

Gifted parents can also feel judged from within the gifted community. Parenting is a tricky and emotional business. Most parents are trying to do the best they can and make the most informed, reasonable choices possible for their own individual child. Often, in an attempt to confirm a person's decision for what is best for their own child, they can try to push their choices on others. Parents would do well to remember that there is great freedom in making decisions for one's own child. You are ultimately in charge, no matter what teachers, administrators, and other parents say or do. You have the right to make whatever choices you need to, without feeling pressured or judged. Try to keep in mind that just because someone makes a different choice does not mean that your choices are wrong—your choice just might be wrong for their child. Remember to exercise caution before offering advice to other parents, and choose your words carefully. A good rule of thumb is to be a patient and supportive listener and withhold any suggestions until the other person expressly asks you for your opinions.

 Fact

Parents can visit Supporting the Emotional Needs of the Gifted for more help and support on parenting your gifted child. You will find interesting articles, links to great parenting resources, and online webinars you can attend. For more information, visit *www.sengifted.org.*

Dealing with judgmental thoughts is particularly difficult since the concerns may actually at times be warranted. As parents, it is important to try to believe the best of other parents, however you may experience some jealous or spiteful people in your parenting journey. In these situations, should they arise, gifted parents have to fight against misconceptions about what it means to raise a gifted child. While you can do all you can to advocate and inform, some people will continue to form false opinions and offer unwanted advice regarding what you are doing wrong. The best solution in these situations is simply walk away. Parents cannot correct all the prejudice nor solve all the ignorance in the world. You can only do what you can when you are presented with opportunities. After that, you need to let it go and move on to keep from being consumed with the need for vindication or validation. Let your validation come from raising a happy, healthy, gifted child who will do great things in life.

Frustrated

Gifted parents express a variety of frustrations. Typically, parents express frustration with their school options. While some areas have many excellent options, others seem to have few, if any. Just the limited number of programs and spaces available within good schools can be frustrating. It is also difficult to get accurate information about those programs once you learn which are available in your area. Many parents struggle with finding out about what resources are available for their child, how to be placed on waiting lists, or getting multiple children into the same school or program. Even in areas with a variety of school choices, parents can struggle with knowing what the best fit is for their child.

Additionally, parents can feel frustrated by the lack of knowledge and resources available for parents of the gifted. While the field has come a long way in the past several decades, there is still a shockingly small body of resources for parents, children, and educators to draw from. Parents can become frustrated when trying to find out more about their child's needs or find opportunities to address special concerns. Parents can find some relief by working together with other gifted parents or their school's gifted specialists. As parents build a network of fellow gifted supporters, they can work together to find services, programs, and information. Thankfully, the online era has ushered in access to information never before known for gifted parents.

Finally, and most difficult for most parents to accept, gifted parents can feel frustrated with their own child. It is difficult to raise any child, let alone a gifted child. Because of the misconception that raising gifted children is easy, parents feel like they cannot share their frustrations over the tremendous task of raising their spirited individual. They can feel frustrated by the constant whirlwind of emotions their child feels. Each day ends in exhaustion, only to do it all over again the next day. Parents of the gifted can also feel frustrated by the extra effort that goes into answering questions and addressing the many passions of a gifted child. Parents can even feel frustrated that their child is not like every other child.

These frustrations are very normal and common to gifted parents. Just knowing that can be a comfort to the parent frustrated from trying to do it all. One helpful strategy to deal with emotions is journal writing. Parents can write out the day's experiences and feelings, letting them go as they write them. It is particularly helpful to look back on those journal entries a week, a month, a year down the road to see your growth as well as your child's progress.

Afraid

All parents face a certain degree of fear on behalf of their children. This is true for parents of the gifted as well. There are many things to fear in addition to the typical worries of a parent. Parents of the gifted often fear not being able to help their child reach his potential. They feel a responsibility for their child's success and worry that their own shortcomings may affect their child's future. Take comfort in knowing that you are the very best parent for your child because you are the parent he has been given. You have the unique skills and talents best suited for that child. Your gifted child may be an expert in a multitude of subjects, but you are an expert at your gifted child. The only credentials you really need are endless love and a healthy dose of patience.

Parents of the gifted also fear not being able to address all the needs of their child. There is a complex web of social and emotional concerns as well as the intellectual. All parents want their children to be happy, but parents of the gifted worry especially about their child's emotional well being. Will they have friends at school? Will the teacher appreciate their quirkiness or will it get them in trouble? Will they find someone to marry one day? Will they find a career that suits them? These are just a few of the worries about the social aspects of parenting gifted kids that are common to parents.

 **Question**

How can parents help fight against the fears that overcome them?
Parents have to work hard to let go of the fears that they cannot control and focus on those that they can. It is important to learn as much as you can about gifted children, put into practice the strategies that will help your child in all her areas of need, and then free her up to be a child with all the bumps and bruises that come along with childhood to shape her into an adult one day. Focusing on building resilience and handling situations as they come can provide a degree of freedom from a parent's fears.

Some parents of the gifted are fearful for their marriages and the wellness of the rest of the family. A gifted child takes so much time and energy that many other areas in the family begin to suffer. Parents work so hard at meeting the needs of their child that sometimes the marriage can take a backseat. Parents should be on guard against this, making sure to take time together and with their other children. Gifted children will take all that you are willing to give without even realizing it; that is just part of their nature. Set reasonable limits and boundaries for your gifted child that allow you and your spouse to spend quality time together and alone time with each of your other children as well.

Finally, parents of the gifted fear for their child's independence, in both the short term and long term. They wonder if the world will accept them for who they are. They are concerned about how their child will handle new environments without their protection. They fear that their child will make mistakes, face obstacles, and possibly, experience failures.

Parents can help their children and themselves by allowing their children to take developmentally appropriate risks from an early age. Young gifted students can begin with approaching someone at the playground, calling a friend on their own for a play date, or attending an event with a friend's family. Older gifted students can become involved in a club, volunteer at a community service event, or attend an outing with friends, unchaperoned. As you guide your child through these encounters with a helpful push from the nest, along with your unconditional support and guidance, you build a safe landing place. You are laying a foundation for guidance and communication that you will continue to build on that will, hopefully, last through your child's lifetime. Your child will have bumps, hurt feelings, and failures along her path, but you can be there to pick her up and help her back on the path. If you wait too long to build that foundation, your child may never learn those necessary skills for independence, and you will miss out on opportunities to build strength into your parent-child relationship.

Overwhelmed

There is a lot to take in and take account for when raising a gifted child. They are, in a word, intense. Raising a gifted child is an all-consuming task that threatens to completely take over a parent's life.

Managing their academic needs, emotional needs, out-of-school activities, and more can become a full-time job. Add in the fact that gifted children seem to need less sleep plus their constant questions and consuming passions, and most parents are ready for a vacation practically every week. Most people do not understand quite what it is like to be responsible for such a dynamic and enthusiastic individual twenty-four hours a day. And that is just for parents who have one gifted child!

Some parents find it helpful to occasionally take time for themselves, away from their children. This can allow parents to reconnect as a couple. Schedule regular date nights with your spouse or partner where you promise not to talk about the children. Consider finding a hobby that you do just for yourself, take time regularly to enjoy nature, or join a book club at your local library. A parent should also maintain a healthy diet and a regular exercise routine, which will keep you in high spirits and model positive living choices for your child. You can take time to pursue your own passions and share them with your family to show how you balance the pursuit of your hobbies with work and family successfully. While it may sound silly or selfish, these activities, done in moderation, can help set an example for your child of what a well-rounded life looks like. By modeling positive lifestyle habits, you are helping your child do the same now and in the future, when she is an adult herself.

 Fact

It is a long-accepted fact that gifted children seem to require less sleep. However, in recent years, some studies have shown that most children—gifted included—are not actually getting enough sleep. It might be helpful to build regular down time into your child's schedule after he is past the age of naps. Down time can consist of whatever you would like it to, but is usually quiet activities done alone like working on puzzles, reading books, or doing quiet building activities. This down time may facilitate needed sleep, and may also give your child a time to rest as well as provide a break for an overwhelmed parent.

It is important for parents to work together to build the family as a unit instead of individual parts. You should strive to pursue family activities together as opposed to activities revolving around the gifted kid. You may consider going on a family picnic, serving in a ministry in church together, or going hiking on the weekend. This is a good way for the gifted child to learn not to monopolize your time by seeing that other people in the family need your time, too. Having a large family can be a blessing this way. The gifted child is forced, by the nature of family dynamics, to realize that he needs to share the attention and time. Parents of only children need to be cautious not to let the family revolve solely around their child, in the same way parents with only one gifted child need to make certain the gifted child is not consuming the time and energies to the detriment of the rest of the family.

The Future

Life may be going along well right now for a gifted child, but parents are always looking to the future. Who will their teacher be next year? What school will they go to? What activities will help them get into college? Are they doing enough extracurricular activities? Are they doing too many extracurricular activities? Parents can spend an inordinate amount of time planning for the future.

While there is nothing wrong with looking forward, parents need to be watchful. First, make sure that you are not spending so much time working out everything in the future that you are failing to enjoy right now. Gifted children are consuming and exhausting, but they are also exciting and interesting to be around. Take the time to delight in your child; eighteen years will slip past before you know it and you will be left wondering where that quirky little child has gone, although you will hopefully have built a strong relationship that will continue to grow even after your child has ventured into the world.

Furthermore, be sure when you are planning the future to take into account your child and her desires. It is easy for parents to get into the habit of making all the decisions for their child; however, it is important to remember to give your child a voice. Allowing her to be a part of the discussion from an early age teaches her decision-making skills as well as how to be flexible and compromise. Most parents will make many of the important decisions for their child when she is young, but starting in mid-elementary school, gifted children can become frustrated if their voice is not heard as choices are being made. The final say can be left up to the parents, but by including your child, you are teaching valuable life skills and perhaps minimizing later rebellions when she is of an age to be making important decisions. Think to the future then; do you want your child to include you and hear your voice as well? Build communication and collaboration into your relationship now if you want to be able to rely upon it in the future.

 **Essential**

One helpful family practice to develop communication skills with your child is posing pretend scenarios or dilemmas. Talking through artificial problems can help your child practice how to handle dilemmas and conflicts. Observing and listening to how he deals with these conflicts helps you to evaluate how much decision-making power you will gradually allow him to have as he grows and matures over the years. If you have trouble coming up with your own scenarios, check out *Dilemmas in a Jar* from Free Spirit Publications.

How to Build a Parent Peer Group

Parents can look to many different sources for help when they need it. Talk with your child's school or district gifted coordinator about opportunities for parent book groups or other activities. They may also be able to provide direction for local gifted activities. There are many parent support groups online for those raising gifted children. Some find it helpful to join or start a local parent support group. Many of these have monthly socials where parents can talk and collaborate while children form friendships. Parents can also meet other gifted parents through special enrichment programs outside of school that their children may be involved in. Gifted specialists around the country also offer counseling and consultations in person, over the phone, or through the Internet for parents who would like an extra degree of support.

Be cautious in choosing a gifted group. Many gifted groups can turn into a group of moms sitting around bragging about their children and their accomplishments. This is not always helpful for parents. Groups that are not structured and purposeful can quickly degenerate into this type of activity, which does not help parents or improve the community view of parents of the gifted. Sitting in a group hearing about how Johnny started reading at two and is now reading seven novels a day can lead parents to have the wrong attitude and become competitive.

Look for a group that has a speaker schedule, reviews current books or literature on giftedness, or plans group activities for parents and children to avoid joining a group that may not be helpful for you.

Getting Help When You Need It

While it may feel like you are alone, it is important to remember that you are not. There are many resources available to parents who are feeling especially overwhelmed as a parent of a gifted child. Additionally, if a school is failing to meet the needs of a child and all avenues of support have been exhausted, a parent may feel the need to bring in an outside gifted specialist to advocate on behalf of their child. These can be found through gifted parent groups, local gifted organizations, another school district, or possibly through online websites for the gifted.

The unique needs of a gifted child sometimes require special services outside of school, as well. Many families can benefit from counseling provided by a professional trained in dealing with the special concerns that gifted families face. If you feel your child is at risk for depression, an eating disorder, or other problems due to their giftedness, it is helpful to seek out family or individual counseling services. Some parents also experience great comfort and support from attending counseling or support groups together, without their child.

Alert

Would you like to start a parent group in your own area? Supporting the Emotional Needs of the Gifted (SENG) has many helpful resources. Several years ago, they developed a procedure for creating an effective local parent support group along with helpful guides and tools. Find out more about these resources on their website at *www .sengifted.org/parents_groups.shtml.*

When in the midst of the storm of parenting, try to remember that this is a light and momentary affliction. What feels all-consuming right now will be over far too soon. As you take it one day at a time, find help and support where you can while embracing your special window of time to raise your unique child.

CHAPTER 7

What about School?

One of the most difficult decisions for any parent of a gifted child to make is where to have their child schooled. For some parents, there are many schools to choose from: charter, public, private. For others, their geographical location limits their opportunities considerably. Parents struggle to make this choice, feeling that the weight of their child's academic success hinges upon making this decision correctly. This chapter will look at the benefits and drawbacks of a variety of educational options for parents of gifted students.

School Options

Parents traditionally had only one choice for schooling their child. Most children went to the local public school in their neighborhood and were educated in a classroom with students of the same age. A child only attended a different school if their family moved.

Now, parents have a broad range of schools available. They can choose their local public school. Some school districts allow them to attend any school in the district, if they are willing to provide transportation. Still others offer magnet schools that provide a specific type of instruction and may or may not be affiliated with a public school system. Many areas have local charter schools that run independent of a school district. Additionally, private and parochial schools continue to be available in some areas. Finally, parents have traditionally had the option of homeschooling their children, although it has been illegal in some states at certain times in the past. Following is an examination of each of these options with the various advantages and disadvantages to each.

Public School Classroom

Public school has existed in a variety of forms in the United States since the 1600s. At that time, it was available primarily to the wealthy and varied from state to state as well as institution to institution. It was not available to all Americans until the end of the nineteenth century. Since then, public school has gone through dramatic changes. Not the least of these includes the passing of the National Defense of Education Act in 1958, requiring options for gifted education. Additionally, the Jacob Javits Gifted and Talented Students Education Act brought new and important research to the forefront of education. Since that time, public school programs for the gifted have continued to advance, making public schooling a viable option for parents deciding where to place their gifted children for schooling.

Public School Self-Contained

One option within the public school system is a self-contained classroom. In a self-contained classroom, students testing with a certain level of giftedness are removed from the regular classroom setting and then placed within a classroom containing only gifted children. Some variations include gifted classes within regular schools, magnet schools where all the classes are gifted, and multi-age-level gifted classrooms.

There are many advantages to a self-contained classroom for your gifted child. They include a classroom inhabited by like-minded and similar children to your own, well-trained teachers prepared to address the complex needs of a gifted child, access to resources for differentiated instruction, and a community of parents who understand what each other is experiencing.

A self-contained classroom is not without its disadvantages, as with all programs. Some parents fear that children will not learn to interact with students who are not gifted. Other parents are concerned that students may have to switch schools in order to participate in these programs, which separates them from their neighborhood friends. Sometimes students can become isolated from the general school population, at times may be placed in separate schools from the siblings based on program space availability, and may become prideful about their intellectual standing.

Public School Pull-Out Program

A very common form of gifted services is a pull-out model. In this model, students who test as gifted are enrolled in a regular education classroom for the majority of their time. They are then pulled out of the classroom for special services. These services could include receiving additional instruction in the area where they are gifted. Sometimes, all gifted students, regardless of their area of giftedness, are pulled out to receive enrichment programs.

Pull-out programs are wonderful in many ways. Students are recognized as being gifted, which boosts their confidence. Gifted children are able to meet their intellectual peers within their school through the pull-out services. Students have an opportunity to do creative and enriching tasks to break up the otherwise routine day.

Pull-out programs are not without their drawbacks. Many parents feel that the pull-out model does not provide enough of a challenge for students, especially when a school utilizes pull-out programming for enrichment only. Teachers often find the pull-out program to be disruptive to the classroom harmony, as children are coming and going. Parents may worry that students will begin to develop an elitist mentality from being pulled out, and that the children staying in the classroom will struggle with their self-esteem since they are not able to participate in these programs. Also, a gifted child may feel ostracized because they are being pulled-out of the traditional classroom environment. This may make them feel as they are somehow not "normal" like the other children. Pull-out programs can be a great fit for bright or moderately gifted children, as long as parents take these drawbacks into consideration as part of their decision-making process.

Private School

Currently, many states do not have provisions for charter schools as an alternative to public schools. Many parents who are in an area with poor public schools may choose to look at private schools.

Private schools can offer an interesting set of advantages to gifted students. Often, private schools use challenging curriculum not available in public schools. Private schools can also draw a more advanced teaching staff. They typically have substantial resources to draw on for providing for classroom and educational needs. Private schools also have the option of refusing students for whatever reason; an option public and charter schools are not afforded. This means that their schools can be gifted only, which can be a benefit for those looking for a school solely for the gifted. These are just a few of the many advantages a private-school setting can provide.

Private schools have several drawbacks, though. First and foremost, private schools may be outside the budget of many families because of their high tuition costs, although some do offer scholarship programs. In addition, private schools can have fewer sports and club programs than public schools. Students who attend private schools may also have a reduced opportunity and access to scholarship information should they choose to pursue higher education later on. The location of the school may also not be convenient for the family, causing disruption to family life.

Charter School

The first charter schools were established in Minnesota in the 1980s. Charter schools began as alternative schools. Many were for troubled youths while others offered specialized programs in the arts, math and science, sports, or other specialized areas. In the past decades, gifted students have found a refuge in charter schools outside the mainstream education community.

There are many advantages to charter schools for gifted students. Charter schools often have specialized niches within the education community. Many provide special programs for gifted students or a specialized focus on math or science. In addition, class sizes are often smaller. Charter schools can have a greater flexibility and freedom in curriculum that allows for more differentiation for gifted students.

However, charter schools are not without their drawbacks. In a charter school, parents have little opportunity for appeal. If something is not working, they can appeal to the teacher and then to the administration. After that, they are faced with a "like it or leave it" dilemma. Additionally, because charter schools are independent, they often have fewer resources than public schools. They do not have the same extracurricular opportunities including clubs and sports, which are often important to students and families. Most states require charter schools to provide special services for students with learning disabilities, but it is important to look into whether a charter school follows these regulations prior to enrolling. Parents should also investigate the credentials of administrators and educators as well, as many do not require a teaching certificate for instructors.

Homeschooling

More and more often, parents of the gifted are looking to homeschooling as a viable alternative to a traditional school setting.

Many parents who cannot afford a private school but live in an area with ineffective public schools look to homeschooling. Beyond that, many families simply feel that homeschooling is the best fit because of its numerous positive aspects.

These positive aspects include the ability to choose your own curriculum. Homeschooling is the only school option where parents have complete control over their child's curriculum. This means they can choose the type of curriculum as well as the level. Parents are able to allow their children to work at their own rate of learning. Homeschooling affords tremendous flexibility in the mode and method of teaching your child. In addition, homeschooling can utilize unconventional means such as creative field trips or visits to experts in a field. Many areas allow homeschooled children to take classes at the local community college from a young age, where they receive instruction from college-credentialed teachers. These opportunities can allow gifted students to graduate early and move on to collegiate-level studies at a younger age.

Homeschooling also has some negative aspects. Many states have very strict regulations concerning homeschooling, which can make it difficult for parents. Homeschooling also typically requires at least one parent to be at home, making it nearly impossible for parents who both work. Single-parent or dual-income families who are dedicated to homeschooling can find a way to make it work, but it can be tremendously difficult for them. Additionally, many parents find the thought of homeschooling overwhelming in terms of the choices to be made, planning lessons, and creating schedules that are effective. Some parents also feel that homeschooling limits their child's social interactions and thus their social development. In some areas, there may be a negative stigma attached to homeschooling. While more and more families are choosing this as a viable education option, there are still those with prejudice against homeschooling, and many stereotypes exist that may have to be overcome. It is important to note that students who have been homeschooled may also have a difficult transition into the mainstream school environment should a parent choose to stop home-schooling for whatever reason.

Resources for Homeschooling Parents

Parents of homeschooled gifted children can find many resources to help them in educating their gifted child, even without being a part of the local school. Many areas have local gifted support groups that meet regularly. These groups often meet for social activities, but can also meet to host guest speakers or authors. Some of these groups for the gifted even have subchapters for gifted homeschooling groups. Parents can join home schooling cooperatives so that their child can have social learning experiences. There is also a large online community of homeschooling gifted parents available to families who choose this mode of education.

Questions to Ask
Before Making Your Choice

There are several questions that a parent should ask themselves before choosing a school for their child.

What Are the Greatest Benefits to My Child at This School?

With any school, it is important to look at what benefits your child will gain from attending a particular school. This is perhaps the most significant aspect of choosing a school. Many schools offer a variety of programs and opportunities. Make sure that you are evaluating which ones are the best for your own unique and individual child. An origami club is great—if your child loves origami. The same goes for an exceptional math and science program: it is great, as long as your child loves and excels at math and science. As you view schools, make sure that they have the resources you need for your child.

What Are the Downsides to This School for My Child?

Parents can get caught up in the excitement of choosing a school and fail to evaluate the situation fully. With each school you visit, it is important to look at the positives as well as the negatives to allow for a full picture. If you fail to accurately evaluate the negatives, you may end up in a school setting where you are very unhappy after the initial glamour wears off. It is often helpful to talk to parents who have had their children at the particular school you are looking at for several years. They have the insider scoop on what the school is really like and can help you assess both the good and the bad of the school in order to make the most informed decision possible.

Alert

When you are making your pros and cons lists for schools you are considering, keep in mind that all pros are not weighted the same as all cons. You may need to establish a point system to weigh items. Decide on what characteristics of a school are most important to you and which are less important. You want to make sure that you are accurately representing those things that are most important to you in a school setting.

Can I See My Child in This Setting?

Take a tour of the school and imagine what your child would look like sitting in the classroom. Try to determine if this school setting would be a place where you could see your child learning and growing. As you look around, try to picture your child interacting with the types of students you see. Examine the curriculum and resources on display to see if your child would be engaged and interested in them. Ask about extracurricular activities to see if these fit with the interests of your potential student. Talk with and observe teachers to see if their personalities match with your child's learning style and needs. Hopefully, when you find the right school, you will be able to visualize your child right there amongst the other students.

Will My Child Be Able to Form Relationships in This School Setting?

As you evaluate schools, it is important to look at the social and emotional impact of your decision. In whatever school setting you choose, your child should be able to feel comfortable with the teachers, administrators, and the other children. All of these might not be possible in the same school, but parents should look at how many people their child will have to build those important bonds with at each school they evaluate.

How Stable Is the Program?

When you are deciding on a school, you need to look at how stable the gifted program is at the schools you are looking at. This is especially important in states with many charter school options. There is always a new and better school out there each year. However, many of these new schools are very dynamic and subject to frequent change. Some aspects to look at are the staff and student turnover rates. If the teachers and administrators are constantly changing, it is hard to know what you can expect from year to year, and the possibility of dissatisfaction becomes more of a factor. On the other hand, you don't want a program that is completely static and possibly stagnant. As much as possible, you should try to avoid having to move your child too many times during her academic career. Choosing a stable program where you know what to expect from year to year can help alleviate some of these potential traumatic changes.

Alert

It is often helpful for parents to decide first what they are hoping to accomplish by sending their child to school. The decision is usually between academic challenge and social adaptation. Many parents want their children to go to school for their mental stimulation while managing their social skills development at home through outside activities. Others feel the most important aspect of school is learning social adaptation while parents provide additional stimulation at home. Some schools are able to provide students with both, but it is often helpful for parents to decide which is most important before they begin their school search.

For many parents, this information can make the decision even more overwhelming. There are just so many options from which to choose. Other parents are in the position of choosing between lesser evils. Keep in mind that very few, if any, parents will find a school that is perfect. As a parent, remember that you are the most important determining factor in your child's success. Wherever your child goes to school, she will look to you to determine her attitude. Once you make your choice, step back and free yourself from the weight of the decision-making burden. Embrace your decision and model a positive attitude for your child. Your child will most likely have good teachers and bad teachers throughout her academic career. She may even have teachers you think are bad, but come to realize later were good, and vice versa—teachers you thought were wonderful only to realize long term were less effective. These can be important lessons in handling conflict and adversity for your child. Use these experiences to grow yourself and your child. Don't allow your school decision to be an excuse for you or your child to stop learning and growing. Ultimately, the responsibility for that falls upon you as the parent.

CHAPTER 8

Enhancing Programs and Learning Opportunities

T here are quite a few opportunities for parents to find enrichment and learning for their gifted child. For gifted students, enhancing programs can provide an opportunity to meet intellectually challenging peers they might not encounter in the school setting. These programs also provide children a chance to explore the many and diverse interests they may have in all different subjects for which a school may not provide clubs or groups. This chapter will look at a variety of different ways that parents can provide meaningful learning opportunities for their gifted child outside of the school setting.

Purposeful Play Dates

As parents meet more fellow parents of gifted children through parent support groups, school programs, and other areas, they can begin to form a community of like-minded parents. Parents can work together to set up play dates with their gifted children.

Keep in mind that your child's closest playmates might not be children of her own age. Gifted children are drawn to others who share their interests, regardless of chronological age. As your child develops passions for a variety of topics and finds others who share them, you can create playgroups of similar interests. One might be a dinosaur group where children spend time visiting science museums, researching different animals, and visiting local experts in archeology. Children fascinated by science can join together for a weekly discovery group where parents plan interesting experiments geared toward their inclinations. Parents can work together to plan activities designed for these shared interests using their collective resources as opposed to one parent trying to do it all on their own.

Gifted and Talented Programs

Over the years, many wonderful summer programs have been created for gifted students. These programs create an excellent supplement for the school curriculum. Some target core-subject advancement while others provide interesting enrichment opportunities for gifted students. Parents should investigate each of these programs to see if one meets their child's needs. Make sure to do your research early, as the programs have limited space and often fill up early.

Summer Institute for the Gifted

The Summer Institute for the Gifted has been providing summer learning opportunities for the gifted since the early 1980s. Over time, their program has expanded to include partnerships with universities all around the country. The Summer Institute for the Gifted is run out of several prominent universities throughout the United States, including Yale, Princeton, and Bryn Mawr. They have several different programs, which are for students from age four all the way through age seventeen. The have residential, day, and weekend program options. Families who live in close proximity to the host schools may have the option of commuting daily, as well.

Their residential program lasts three weeks. Students live on campus and are instructed in academic areas, while developing social skills and forging friendships that can last a lifetime. The day programs are geared at younger students, aged four through fourteen, who may not be ready to be away from home for such an extended period of time. The day programs include mathematics, science, and recreation classes. Students choose which classes they would like to participate in, and those classes are organized into ninety-minute-long blocks. The weekend program consists of Saturday sessions for students in grades first through sixth. This is another wonderful opportunity for your child to meet like-minded students and be taught by talented and skilled instructors familiar with the unique needs of the gifted. You can find out more about the Summer Institute for the Gifted at their website: *www.giftedstudy.org.*

Duke TIP Program

The Duke University Talent Identification Program (TIP) is run through Duke University in Durham, North Carolina. They also utilize partner universities for their satellite programs to make gifted programming available to children in a variety of geographical locations. Duke TIP provides many different learning opportunities for students from fourth grade through high school.

Duke TIP offers summer residential programs (local families may also commute) and is geared toward students in middle school and high school. Students are hosted by local universities, and participate in rigorous and interesting programs during a three-week stay. In recent years, the program has grown to include field-study opportunities around the world.

Duke TIP also offers Scholar Weekends throughout the year for students in eighth through twelfth grade. The Scholar Weekends provide exciting enrichment opportunities for students in sixteen different states across the country. These weekends are also hosted by colleges and universities.

In addition, Duke TIP hosts eStudies as well as eSeminars for students in grades eight through twelve. These are online distance-learning courses that take place over the summer or throughout the academic school year. The online programs can be the extra enrichment students are looking for!

Finally, Duke TIP offers independent learning courses for students from fourth through twelfth grade. Students enroll in these challenging classes and complete them from the comfort of home. The classes are available in a variety of formats, including CD-ROM, workbook, or online versions. To find out more about the Duke TIP program, visit their website at *www.tip.duke.edu.*

✅ Fact

The Duke Talent Identification Program has been providing quality programs for gifted students as well as talent identification services since 1981. In the twenty years since its inception, Duke TIP talent search has grown from identifying 8,700 students to helping over 71,000 gifted and talented students!

Davidson Institute

The Davidson Institute for Talent Development is a 501(c)3 organization founded in 1999 to provide quality, free programs for profoundly gifted and talented students across the United States. The Davidson Institute offers a variety of programs for gifted students aged eighteen and under. According to Bob Davidson, founder of the Davidson Institute for Talent Development, "The Davidson Institute is built on the belief that individuals who have extraordinary intelligence and talents, when encouraged and supported, can improve the quality of life for us all. The Davidson Institute works with students, parents, educators, and other professionals to ensure that all students are provided an educational experience commensurate with their abilities." The following programs demonstrate this dedication to excellence in the field of gifted education.

Davidson Young Scholars Program

The Davidson Young Scholars program is a free support-service program available to parents of profoundly gifted children aged five through eighteen. The program offers families help with talent development, educational support, and social-emotional skills development. Parents have access to an online support community in addition to annual social gatherings and access to other programs offered through the Davidson Institute. Parents can apply for the Young Scholars program by downloading an application from their website; the application must be submitted with one letter of recommendation.

THINK Summer Institute

The THINK Summer Institute is a three week-long residential program offered to students ages thirteen through sixteen. The program is hosted on the University of Nevada, Reno campus. Students who participate in this exciting course of study also have the opportunity to earn as many as six college credits during their stay.

The Davidson Academy of Nevada

The Davidson Academy of Nevada is a free, public day school for gifted students in Reno, Nevada, opened by the Davidson Institute in 2006. The Academy is free for students whose parents live in the state of Nevada. Students from outside Nevada may still apply to enroll; however, they are subject to tuition as well as room and board fees. Students must meet strict qualification requirements in order to attend. The Davidson Academy does not have set grade levels; students are evaluated based on their abilities and are subsequently placed into appropriate courses. Students and teachers work together to create a learning plan for each student. The Davidson Academy is a unique school program for exceptionally gifted students.

Davidson Fellows

The Davidson Fellows program offers scholarships to extraordinary gifted and talented children aged eighteen and under who completed significant work in the fields of mathematics, science, literature, music, technology, philosophy, and "outside the box." Parents can see examples of previous winners as well as information about applying on the Davidson Institute website. Parents can learn more about the wide range of programs offered by the Davidson Institute as well as apply for them by visiting their website: *www.davidsongifted.org*.

⒠⃝ Alert

To learn more about how the Davidson Institute began, check out the book *Genius Denied: How to Stop Wasting our Brightest Young Minds* by Jan and Bob Davidson. The book contains fascinating information regarding the current state of gifted education in addition to a history of the work the Davidsons are doing within the field of gifted and talented students.

Johns Hopkins Center for Talented Youth

The Johns Hopkins Center for Talented Youth (CTY) is one of the oldest centers for the gifted in existence. In 1972, Dr. Julian Stanley, a psychology professor at The Johns Hopkins University, introduced the first Talent Search designed to identify, challenge, and reward academically able young people. He developed the CTY to help meet the needs of this special population. The program has successfully identified over one million gifted and talented students as well as providing support services to over 100,000 students through their wide range of programs. Students must first be part of the Center for Talented Youth Talent Search. Once they have been identified, students are eligible for the programs offered through CTY.

Summer Programs

CTY provides many summer programs for gifted and talented children in grades two through twelve. CTY offers both residential as well as day programs to students. In the CTY summer program, students take part in challenging courses meant to engage the mind and challenge the thinking of gifted students. The classes are grouped by age, and usually last three weeks. Students can view the course catalog and choose the enrichment classes that appeal to their unique interests and passions.

CTY Online

Johns Hopkins CTY also offers online programs for students wishing to do distance learning. A variety of courses are available for students from preschool through twelfth grade. Courses are available for students who qualify as verbally gifted as well as mathematically gifted. The courses utilize Internet technology to provide content; however, they are still interactive between students and instructors. Some of the possible courses for elementary students include Arabic, Chinese, critical reading, and competitive math. Courses for intermediate and high school students include Spanish, java programming, cryptography, and fiction writing as well as many different advanced-placement science and mathematics courses.

 Fact

The CTY Online program was a forerunner in distance learning, having begun their work in the field in 1983. Since that time, the program has served over 10,000 students wishing to receive extra enrichment and challenging coursework—all from their own living room.

Family Academic Programs

The Family Academic Programs were created for students identified as gifted through the Johns Hopkins Talent Search. The programs include gifted children as well as their families. Families are introduced to exciting learning topics in creative settings. Family

Academic Programs opportunities are available for students from second grade through twelfth grade. The programs are hosted in a variety of cities across the nation. Family Academic Program topics include studies taking place at zoos, maritime institutions, and museums.

Parents can visit the Johns Hopkins Center for Talented Youth website for more information about the program as well as steps for application. Their website is *http://cty.jhu.edu.*

Northwestern University Center for Talent Development

The Northwestern Center for Talent Development (CTD) began in 1982, and has continued to be a leader in research on and identification of gifted children. In addition to these two areas, they also provide many programs for gifted students.

Summer Programs

The Northwestern CTD Summer Programs have been operating for more the twenty-five years. The CTD Summer Programs provide residential or commuter programs to students from preschool through twelfth grade. Students participate in academically challenging and exciting programs over the course of three weeks during the summer. The program is hosted by Northwestern University on their campus in Evanstown, Illinois.

Weekend Enrichment Programs

Northwestern CTD also offers Saturday and Weekend Enrichment courses for gifted and talented students. The Saturday and Weekend Enrichment program offers a wide variety of engaging courses for students who wish to receive additional enrichment. The program has classes for students from preschool through ninth grade. Courses are hosted throughout the state of Illinois at a variety of locations.

Gifted Learning Links

Gifted Learning Links gives students in kindergarten through twelfth grade the opportunity to take challenging courses online through the Northwestern Center for Talent Development. Students can take enrichment courses or participate in college or advance-placement courses with the potential to receive college credit upon course completion.

Another interesting component are the online Family Courses offered for students in kindergarten through second grade. Family Courses last nine weeks and engage the entire family in exciting enrichment learning.

All of the Gifted Learning Links courses provide a variety of assignments and extension activities in addition to online real-time discussions where students and families are given the chance to interact with other gifted families like themselves.

Civic Education Project

The Civic Education Project is an innovative program that unites community involvement with interactive education. Students in grades seven through twelve spend three weeks during the summer learning leadership as well as civic mindedness as they complete projects on the campus of Northwestern University. In addition to the skills built, students can form lasting friendships with other gifted and talented youth.

If you are interested in learning more about the programs offered by Northwestern Center for Talent Development, visit their website at *www.ctd.northwestern.edu.*

⚠ Alert

Stanford's Educational Program for Gifted Youth

Stanford Educational Program for Gifted Youth (EPGY) started in 1963 as an extension of a computer-based mathematics program. They have since grown into an ongoing research program devoted to the creation of online curriculum for gifted students in grades six through twelve. They currently serve thousands of students each year through their online and in-person programs.

EPGY Online Program

Stanford's Educational Program for Gifted Youth (EPGY) is perhaps one of the most developed online programs for gifted and talented children. The program has served over 50,000 students from locations around the world since it was founded. The programs are offered to students in grades kindergarten through twelve across a variety of disciplines. The program offers self-paced courses as well as courses that require more interactive involvement. Some of the courses offered include accelerated grade-level mathematics, computer programming, and Latin, among others. Many parents have successfully substituted the Stanford online curriculum for their child's traditional program of study in a regular education classroom as an accommodation for a gifted student. Parents can find out more information as well as explore the course catalog and sign up for classes on their website at *http://epgy.stanford.edu*.

Stanford EPGY Online High School

The Stanford EPGY Online High School offers a program like no other for gifted students in seventh through twelfth grade. The program is fully accredited, and able to provide diplomas to students who "attend" this completely online high school. "The mission of EPGY OHS is to provide a stimulating and challenging education that equips and inspires talented students to academic and professional success." Gifted students have the opportunity to enroll in a variety of course loads, either full time or part time. The coursework is rigorous and challenging, exactly what a gifted middle or high school student needs. As part of the high school program, students can also attend residential programs on the Stanford campus.

Stanford EPGY Summer Institutes

Stanford EPGY Summer Institutes are offered as a residential program on the Stanford Campus in Palo Alto, California. The programs consist of two- to four-week sessions for students in grades six through twelve. Students have the opportunity to take part in challenging coursework including a variety of subjects such as engineering, business, and bioscience. The Summer Institute offers classes most students would not be able to take at their local high school, in addition to the opportunity to work with fellow gifted and talented students from across the nation.

Question

How do we know which program is right for our child?
To make the best decision for your family, first look at what programs are available based on your child's age and grade. Then take into account where programs are located as well as the dates that they are offered. After programs have been ruled out based on these criterion, evaluate the remaining programs based on your budget, your child's interest levels, and the commitment involved.

These are just a few of the programs available nationwide. You may find other programs by talking to parents you know or through your school's gifted department or through your own research online.

Online Programs

For parents unable to participate in on-site programs, online programs provide a viable option. Several of the organizations above have online components to their programs. In addition, many other institutions specialize in online programs for gifted and talented students.

OnlineG3

OnlineG3 is an online curriculum program with courses in the humanities primarily. Students can enroll in a variety of courses that provide an enriching and engaging curriculum. OnlineG3 classes are geared toward interests and abilities, without constraints of a student's age. Their courses encourage creativity, problem solving, and logical thinking—the hallmarks of gifted education. Parents can find out more at *www.onlineg3.com*.

Vision Learning

Vision Learning is a comprehensive online curriculum that is free for students. Their courses are primarily mathematics and science based. The content can be used to supplement already existing studies in order to provide an additional challenge and exposure to more complex content. To learn more, visit their website at *www.visionlearning.com*.

Assessment and Learning in Knowledge Spaces (ALEKS)

Assessment and Learning in Knowledge Spaces is a completely internet-based curriculum program. ALEKS is particularly interesting in that it is an artificially intelligent curriculum program.

This allows the program to quickly and continually assess student knowledge in order to ensure fresh, challenging content each time a student is working. ALEKS is an excellent supplement to an existing curriculum. They offer programs from kindergarten through twelfth grade. The topics covered include mathematics, business, and science, among others. Learn more about the ALEKS program as well as registration specifics on their website: *www.aleks.com.*

These are just a few of the online programs available to gifted students. The Internet has greatly increased the accessibility of enrichment and advancement programs. Parents can find a comprehensive list of distance-learning program options available at Hoagies' Gifted website: *www.hoagiesgifted.org/distance_learning .htm.* With a little bit of research, parents looking to provide extra challenge from the comfort of home can find a program that fits their child and their family's needs.

Community Enrichment Programs

Another option for parents is community programs. While these are not typically geared toward gifted students, they can provide much-needed enrichment for students. You can start by checking out the programs offered by your city or county parks and recreation department. They usually have a catalog offering programs like arts and crafts, cooking, or sports. You can also check through your local library for youth book clubs. If your child has a particular niche, you may be able to find a group or organization that hosts programs for youth. An excellent example of this would be youth acting troupes. Most cities have acting companies that offer youth programs throughout the year and over the summer. Additionally, your child's school may pass out information on programs affiliated with or offered by the school district. While these programs most likely won't challenge your child academically, they can provide stimulation based on their passion that may be exactly what your child needs to help them feel as though they are growing and learning.

Gifted children are usually not satisfied simply by their school program of study. Their diverse interests require careful cultivation. Exposing them to challenging programs and interesting enrichment helps in the development of the whole child. Through programs like those shared in this chapter, gifted children can learn valuable life skills and gain important social and emotional experiences. On top of that, they often provide fun for the whole family!

CHAPTER 9

Twice-Exceptional Children

Children who are identified as being gifted as well as having a learning disability are commonly referred to as twice exceptional. This term also applies to children who have a twice exceptionality along the lines of a behavioral disorder or other diagnosable conditions. It is not uncommon for a child who is highly gifted to also have some type of disability or disorder. This chapter will look at some of the most common forms of twice-exceptional children.

What Is Twice Exceptional?

Twice-exceptional children are typically identified first as being gifted, and then later, a learning disability or behavioral disorder is diagnosed. This pattern is typical because giftedness commonly masks a learning disability in the early elementary school years. Children with disabilities can compensate very well for a long time. Many can even make it to high school or college before their disability is recognized, if ever. The gifted brain is a marvelous instrument, accomplishing its purposes no matter the difficulty!

Behavioral disorders are also secondary discoveries for many gifted children. Often, educators and care providers dismiss the issues because of a child's giftedness. This is especially true for those who may have some knowledge of the behaviors associated with being gifted. However, most professionals with training in working with the gifted will be able to spot a behavioral disorder and steer parents toward proper care and treatment.

Sometimes, parents of children with an already diagnosed behavioral condition or learning disability recognize that there is something different about their child—beyond what has been diagnosed. It can be particularly difficult for parents in this situation to get their child tested for a gifted program or services. Parents should continue to pursue the matter, though, even to the point of outside testing, if necessary. There are many, many twice-exceptional children out there, all of whom deserve the complete range of services necessary for their optimum individual learning potential.

Why It's Twice as Hard as a Parent

Parents of children who are twice exceptional face an added degree of difficulty in parenting. They have to juggle the trials of parenting a gifted child while also navigating the special education services side of education. These parents can feel easily overwhelmed with all of the information and meetings required to help their child. Many times, people may be reticent to give a gifted diagnosis because of a learning disability or behavioral disorder. They may also think that because a child has been identified as gifted they are immune to learning disabilities or behavioral disorders. Parents must educate themselves on what it means to be twice exceptional at the same time as they are advocating for the needs of the gifted, the learning disabled, and those with behavioral disorders.

Twice-exceptional parents face the challenges of both gifted parents and of parents of special needs children. This doubles the confusion, judgment, frustration, and most certainly the sense of being overwhelmed by their child's needs. There can be an endless maze of bureaucracy for both issues in order to ascertain all the necessary therapies and accommodations required by their child.

Fact

Although research is not conclusive, studies done in the early part of the past decade identified more than 70,000 children who are twice exceptional within the public school systems. It is a comfort to parents to know that they are certainly not alone in this endeavor.

Twice Exceptional with Learning Disabilities

Many children who are gifted can also be diagnosed with a variety of learning disabilities. This is not uncommon amongst the gifted. The brain makes choices all the time. As it is choosing to direct energy and resources toward an area of giftedness, it diverts those resources away from other areas. When this is particularly severe, a child can be determined to have a learning disability—typically in the area opposite of their greatest strength area. Many researchers believe that the greater the level of giftedness, the greater the deficit can be in another area. In order to determine a disability, teachers and education specialists look at both a child's intelligence tests as well as their school work. A child is considered to have a learning disability when there is a significant disparity between their IQ level and their performance ability. If a child has a high intelligence level but is consistently failing to perform parallel to that level, schools and care providers begin to look at the possibility of a learning disability.

 **Essential**

> Learning disabilities are usually grouped based on the area of disability. They are typically considered reading disabilities, writing disabilities, or mathematical disabilities. If you are concerned your child may have a learning disability, begin by looking at which areas of their work are showing problems starting with the following three areas as a guide.

One of the most important tools against a learning disability is early detection. Your child being identified as gifted is not an inoculation against a learning disability. Parents should be watchful from a young age for areas of unreasonable difficulty or possible lagging skills. Seeking out a trained professional to provide intervention and special services can make a huge difference in your child's future academic success as a gifted student who also has a learning disability.

Dyslexia

One common area for gifted children to have a learning disability is dyslexia. Dyslexia is a disability that relates to a child's reading. Early symptoms include difficulty learning to read and commonly reversing letters.

Dyslexia comes in a variety of forms, as it is used broadly to identify reading disorders. It can include children who are able to read but unable to comprehend. These are children who may have learned to memorize words without actually sounding them out or learning the rules of phonics. Additionally, dyslexia can refer to children who can read words that follow common phonetic patterns but not those that are irregular. Finally, some dyslexic children can identify related words, but not the actual word that is in the text that they are reading (for example, interchanging "dog" for the written word "puppy").

✅ Fact

Parents should also be aware that reversing letters can be developmental. Many children reverse letters and numbers as they are beginning to gain an understanding of written language. Reversals on their own are not a cause to worry, unless they continue past the time when a child is reading and writing fluently. Reversals are something to be aware of, but also to evaluate within the scope of your child's total abilities and skills.

Parents of very young gifted children should be particularly on guard for signs of dyslexia. Many gifted children begin to "read" at a very young age. Make sure that your child is actually learning the phonetic sounds that accompany learning to read and not simply memorizing words. Gifted children can often mask a reading disability such as dyslexia through memorization and well-meaning parents miss this in their pride over their child reading so early. Try to discourage your child from memorization by providing a variety of interesting books and changing them frequently. It is critical to receive help for their disability as early as possible.

Dyspraxia

Dyspraxia is a learning disability that affects the brain's message sending to the motor systems of the body. The brain is processing accurately, but the messages are not being sent or received correctly. The two defining characteristics of dyspraxia, according to the Dyspraxia Foundation, are trouble planning a series of movements as well as trouble following through on an action even when the brain understands the motion. Dyspraxia can affect a student's speech, causing them problems with making certain sounds, establishing correct breathing patterns, and forming sentences. It can also affect fine motor skills such as holding a pencil correctly, writing for long amounts of time, and being able to correctly form letters and numbers. Finally, children with dyspraxia can have gross motor skills problems, including difficulty balancing, maintaining proper social distances, and general clumsiness.

🅐 Alert

Dyspraxia can often be misdiagnosed as dyslexia because of the trouble it creates in the fine motor area of development. Children may incorrectly form letters and numbers, also a symptom of dyslexia, because of the difficulty they have processing the movements of writing. If your child is having prolonged difficulty properly forming letters and numbers, make sure to have them tested for both dyslexia and dyspraxia. Proper identification is the key to proper intervention services.

Some of the characteristics with dyspraxia seem to align with the asynchronous development of gifted children. It is important to watch your child's development carefully to know whether there is a general delay in development common with gifted children such as trouble learning to jump rope or swing, or if it applies to all of their fine and gross motor skills, in which case you may decide to pursue testing for dyspraxia.

Dysgraphia

According to the National Institute for Health, dysgraphia, unlike dyspraxia or dyslexia, is a neurological disorder. It is characterized by difficulty with writing-related functions. It is usually caused by a lack of activity in the part of the brain that handles writing functions. Those with dysgraphia typically have trouble making their letters the right size, properly spacing letters, and correctly separating words within sentences. Additionally, they can use odd or creative spellings or replace long words with shorter alternatives. Most individuals with dysgraphia have poor handwriting. All of these can put a young student in a gifted environment under considerable strain, as they are unable to produce work and keep up with demanding requirements.

Treatment for dysgraphia includes exercises to train the brain in motor functions. Many find some degree of help from these treatments, but most of those diagnosed with this disorder will continue to struggle with writing functions. Proper identification can help ensure that a child is placed under appropriate expectations, has reasonable accommodations made at school for their disorder, and receives continuing services to help with their difficulties. This is especially important for gifted children who are given uncommonly high expectation levels that would be particularly frustrating to a child with a learning disability or disorder.

 Alert

> Another disorder to be aware of that has become increasingly more identified is Sensory Integration Disorder. Gifted children are prone to hypersensitivity because of their intensity. However, Sensory Integration Disorder is different in that a child's brain is processing sensory input in a way that is not normal to the actual sensory experience when there is no apparent biological reason for this.

Other Types of Twice Exceptional

Below are some more examples of twice-exceptional situations in gifted children.

ADD/ADHD

Many parents are already familiar with the disorders known as ADD and ADHD. ADD stands for Attention Deficit Disorder while ADHD stands for Attention Deficit/Hyperactivity Disorder. The two are often used interchangeably, and have garnered much press in the last several years.

Many of the characteristics of ADD and ADHD are similar to those of gifted children, which place gifted children at a high risk for being inaccurately diagnosed as having either disorder. Some of the characteristics for ADD/ADHD include poor attention span, lack of impulse control, inability to follow directions, trouble following rules and procedures, restlessness, and failure to complete tasks.

On the other hand, the characteristics commonly associated with giftedness that are similar to these are: boredom, propensity for getting lost in his thoughts or daydreaming, lack of common sense, high activity level, trouble submitting to authority, questioning rules that do not make sense, and failure to complete tasks the she considers unimportant.

The differences are very subtle. ADD/ADHD is commonly diagnosed using a behavior survey or a rating scale. A child who is gifted may test very high on the survey simply by demonstrating the behaviors that make them gifted. One of the primary differences, however, is whether or not the behaviors are consistent for ADD/ADHD. Gifted children can demonstrate tremendous focus when they are intrigued by a topic. Children with ADD/ADHD cannot focus without help from medication or intervention strategies while gifted children can often refocus when off task. Many kids find an accurate diagnosis when a parent looks at several settings, for example at school, karate class, and church. If the child cannot sustain focus or manage their actions in any of those settings, they may actually have one of the disorders. Gifted children are also often daydreaming or off task because they know that they have achieved mastery at a skill or may have already completed the task, and the teacher does not realize that they are ready to move on. Often, a lack of motivation can masquerade as ADD/ADHD for gifted children who prefer to be personally invested before demonstrating their performance skills.

Teachers are often quick to label children as ADD/ADHD when they cause problems in the classroom. As you can see from the list of characteristics above, children with these behaviors can be very distracting and cause problems in the classroom. Often, educators and parents are looking for a quick fix to help restore balance in school and at home. Parents should be very careful to do extensive research and seek at least one alternate assessment before allowing their child to be diagnosed as ADD/ADHD when they have already been identified as gifted.

There are gifted children that do actually have ADD/ADHD. Many of these children can benefit from medications available from your pediatrician or child psychologist. Some parents have had success with behavioral training or diet modification. The important thing is to make sure your child gets the help he needs in order to be successful as well as learning strategies that will help throughout his academic career.

Oppositional Defiance

Oppositional Defiance Disorder is a very popular diagnosis for gifted children today. Many gifted children demonstrate their gift-edness in part by questioning authority. However, the behavioral traits for children with ODD, based on the *Diagnostic and Statistical Manual for Mental Disorders*, include but are not limited to regularly arguing, being actively defiant, refusing to follow rules, deliberately annoying others, and acting spitefully or vindictively. A gifted student, on the other hand, usually annoys people without intending to or realizing they have done so. They do not defy all adults; often they simply defy the adults they feel are not intellectual peers. Gifted children will follow rules that make sense to them and have been explained. Additionally, a gifted child is often an excellent debater—not arguing simply to argue but to make a point or defend a position. Gifted children are highly passionate with a clearly defined sense of right and wrong. When they feel that code has been violated, their passion will take over. Adults who are not used to such behaviors often interpret this as defiance.

A child with ODD will not be able to change their behaviors when reasoned with or when the situation is explained. However, a gifted child will most likely be able to correct their behavior or apologize for offending others once the situation is properly explained to them. Parents can usually work with their gifted child on a few behavior-modification strategies to correct the issues they are having. They can also discuss with teachers and care providers strategies for working with gifted children that may help relieve additional burdens on their child. If these tactics do not help to remedy the situation, parents may choose to investigate a diagnosis of ODD for their gifted child.

This is considered an anger disorder. Some others commonly recognized/diagnosed/discussed in current gifted communities include Conduct Disorder, Intermittent Explosive Disorder, and Narcissistic Personality Disorder.

Asperger's Syndrome and Giftedness

Asperger's Syndrome is a developmental disorder known to cause difficulties in a person's ability to communicate with others and interact socially. Asperger's Syndrome is currently considered a part of autism. Autism is a spectrum disorder, meaning those diagnosed with this disorder are placed on a continuum of sorts, depending on the severity of their symptoms. Those with high-functioning processes are able to live as successful members of their families and communities despite their autistic tendencies. Some of the symptoms of Asperger's include engaging in long, completely one-sided discussions or debates, poor nonverbal communication (inability to maintain eye contact, difficulty standing still, lack of facial responses, strange or inappropriate hand and body gestures) as well as inability to understand humor or display empathy for others. While there is no cure for Asperger's Syndrome, treatment and behavioral coaching can lessen the symptoms and help those suffering with Asperger's to fit better into their social spheres.

Fact

Asperger's has actually been a formal diagnosis since the 1960s, and is named after an Austrian doctor who first studied the syndrome. Since that time, research on this disorder has continued, providing tremendous advancements in the way Asperger's is treated.

Due to the growing awareness of autism as well as Asperger's Syndrome, many children are being diagnosed with this syndrome and are receiving the help that they need to become successful in their academic and social development. Unfortunately, this means misdiagnosis has also grown. Asperger's, like many of the other disabilities and disorders discussed here, have some similar characteristics to giftedness. It has become something of a catchall for anyone who is bright but also socially awkward. While it is true that some socially awkward people have Asperger's Syndrome, it is not a one-size-fits-all diagnosis.

The symptoms for Asperger's, according to the *Diagnostic and Statistical Manual for Mental Disorder*, include impaired social interactions (lack of eye contact, inability to make friends, lack of emotional encounters, and difficulty interpreting the humor and tone of voice of others) and restricted repetitive behaviors (abnormal fascination with one activity, rigid need for schedule, repetitive movements, and preoccupation with parts of items). Children who are gifted as well as children who have Asperger's Syndrome can be clumsy. They can also both be argumentative or defensive of their areas of passion. Some further commonalities between those with Asperger's and those who are gifted are a wonderful memory, inquisitive mind, precise vocabulary, and a preoccupation with acquiring knowledge on a topic. Children with Asperger's as well as children who are gifted may both exhibit sensory issues. In his book *Misdiagnosis and Dual Diagnoses of Gifted Children and Adults*, Dr. James Webb shares a two-pronged test for differentiating between giftedness and Asperger's. First, introduce the child to those who share his interests. A gifted child will be able to forge common bonds over this shared interest while a child with Asperger's will not be able to create a relationship even with a joint passion. For the secondary test, parents can look at how their child responds to another child's behavior. Gifted children know that they are awkward and that others perceive them that way, while a child with Asperger's is genuinely unaware of how others perceive him. While this does not provide a comprehensive medical diagnosis, which should only come from a trained mental health care provider, it can provide enough information to allay a parent's fears.

❗ Alert

An excellent resource for parents wishing to learn more about twice-exceptional children is *Misdiagnosis and Dual Diagnoses of Gifted Children and Adults* by Dr. James T. Webb, et al. It was written by a series of authors with extensive credentials in the mental health field as well as the field of gifted education. Educators and gifted specialists alike find a great deal of help and support services through this excellent resource. Parents can find more information on this book in the additional resources section.

These are simply the most common disabilities and disorders talked about within the gifted community today. There are a variety of other disabilities and disorders that could not be included, as this is not a book exclusively on twice-exceptional children. If you feel your child has issues not discussed here, make sure to seek out further resources such as those mentioned in the appendix, or seek help from your child's primary care provider.

CHAPTER 10

Social and Emotional Awareness

One of the most common areas for concern amongst gifted parents is the importance of understanding a gifted child's social and emotional needs. Many parents worry about this far more than they worry about their child's academic needs. The social and emotional needs of gifted children are uniquely different from other children, and require special attention because of that uniqueness.

Issues Facing Gifted Children

The brain of a gifted child works in such a way as to cause them to be very keen to certain stimuli. Most of the issues facing children in the social sphere relate to this oversensitivity. Gifted children are usually very perceptive and understanding and have a complex humor and higher-level reasoning. Adults get so used to this perceptiveness being correct that they sometimes don't notice when it is not, or when a child is overly sensitive to the point of trouble. Gifted children sometimes perceive a slight or criticism where none is intended. They can also internalize honest evaluation, replaying it over and over in their heads *ad naseum*. Additionally, gifted children can also suffer from asynchronous development, causing their brains to be immaturely developed in handling certain social situations. These issues are at the root of the social and emotional struggle of gifted children.

Asynchronous Development

Asynchronous development refers to the development of gifted children happening out of step with their chronological or intellectual age. While gifted children often appear very mature to others because they can understand complex topics and converse easily with adults, they are still children. At times, because of their advanced intellectual abilities, they may even be behind in their social skills. Their brain simply does not take the time to process the social cues and train itself to act accordingly. This results in its own set of social issues for gifted children. Parents can become frustrated because their child whines beyond preschool, cries easily into middle school, or is wary of strangers through elementary school. These are simply examples of a natural manifestation of asynchronous development that parents have to work harder at longer than other parents whose children are on a more traditional social and emotional growth path. Every child is different and learns at a different rate. Remind yourself that all children have struggles in some areas, but the majority grow out of them to be successful adults with the help and training of their parents. Also, try to remember that nothing can be done to change a child's rate of development. You can help train your child in healthy social and emotional responses, but you cannot make their brain grow faster. This should provide some comfort to parents currently overwhelmed by this stage.

Common Concerns

Having an understanding of how gifted children develop differently with regard to their social and emotional development often prompts concerns amongst parents. These concerns take on a variety of forms and have equally diverse ways of being addressed. The concerns about gifted children's social and emotional development can take on a variety of faces. Many are related to their high level of sensitivity. Some are related to their keen introspection. Still others are related to their logical and deductive abilities. Navigating these issues can be challenging for a parent.

Dreams Versus Reality

Gifted children are very intellectual. They are dreamers and creators. Gifted children can become very frustrated when they are not able to find a balance between their creativity and their actual abilities. In the school setting, this can become a problem as children recognize their own limitations and refuse to settle for anything less. They get angry, appear unmotivated, or act out toward the teacher. Parents can help children by explaining to them what is happening in a clear and practical way. Knowledge is often the key to getting through to a gifted child. Saying something like, "I understand that you want to write a book with many chapters and a complex plot like the book you are currently reading because that is what you understand a story to be. You are free to do that in your own time, but right now, you need to demonstrate that you understand how to write a story with all the parts of a plot that is only one page long. After you have completed that, you may move on to your novel."

Social Concerns

Gifted children can also be very aware of social concerns. Ideas of war, homelessness, poverty, and more can become very painful to them, as they strongly empathize with others and take their pain into themselves. They may become pained to the point of losing sleep over these and other issues. Children who were born after September 11th can still be deeply pained by the anniversary as they imagine the pain felt by others on that day. Parents can help children by openly and honestly discussing how they are feeling without trivializing or belittling the intensity of their emotions. It is good to remember that while a gifted child may seem to be particularly dramatic, their emotions are very real to them.

Many children find solace in providing aid of some sort: organizing a food and clothing drive, participating in Meals on Wheels, doing research. However, at the same time, parents should be careful not to allow their children to develop an unhealthy obsession. They should be careful to limit exposure to news footage or images of catastrophic events, as a gifted child's mind may have difficulty letting go of such information. Current research says children in general should not be exposed to graphic visual or audio content. Parents must maintain a delicate balance of helping foster their child's civic awareness as well as protecting them in their fragile youth.

Perfectionism

Perfectionism continues to be a concern for parents of gifted children. Perfectionism can be defined as an unhealthy focus on all aspects of life being perfect, and an inability to cope when those standards are not met. Perfectionism does not just affect a student's schoolwork. Students who struggle with perfectionism can see its effects on their social and emotional development as well, primarily in two ways. Being perfect can become an obsession with no room for error, leaving friends, parents, and everyone else in the wake. A perfectionist child can become so consumed with being perfect that they fail to be accepting of others who do not hold to the same ideals as their own. They can also become insistent that parents and friends meet their high standards—refusing to allow flexibility or freedom for others. This can be very hurtful to relationships with others, as loved ones try to either meet those standards, or deal with the harsh judgments and criticisms of the perfectionist. On the other hand, gifted children who suffer from perfectionism can completely give up for fear of failure should they try. These children can become apathetic and despondent, rarely showing enthusiasm or passion for anything. Children with this manifestation of perfectionism are often labeled as lazy or unmotivated. Many adults in their lives fail to identify fear of failure as the motivation behind their lack of performance, and thus their needs go unaddressed. Parents with children representing either side of perfectionism should seek out help to address perfectionism early.

Inappropriate Social Responses

One of the saddest social behaviors for parents to observe in their gifted child is their inappropriate response to social situations. Gifted children can display this in many ways. They may laugh at the wrong time, too much, or not enough with their peers. They may fail to have dialogue, resorting simply to one-sided soliloquies. Additionally, they may be unable to tell when others are no longer interested—or able to tell but unable to remedy the conversational quandary. Gifted children may fail to make eye contact when speaking with others.

All of these inappropriate social responses can take a toll on a child trying to fit in and forge relationships with others. They can make parents uncomfortable in social settings, as well. Parents can help their child in many ways. Gifted children find tremendous relief in having a subject clearly and logically explained to them. Parents can take any one of these issues and break it down for their child. For example, "When you don't look someone in the eye when you speak to them, they think that you are being rude. It tells them that you don't care about them and are not interested in what they have to say. If you want people to know you're being polite, try to look at their face. You may want to nod periodically when you agree with something they say. Wait to ask questions until they stop, and continue to look at them while you are responding to what they said." It may sound silly to break things down in such a way, but gifted children find such step-by-step instructions hugely helpful in navigating social situations.

🔴 Alert

Eye contact can be a culturally relevant social issue. Many cultures find direct eye contact aggressive and prideful. Make sure to be aware of the cultural aspects of social and emotional interactions that are outside the social norm when you are helping your child learn to relate to others, especially if they attend a school or other gathering where many diverse backgrounds will be represented.

Another helpful strategy that cannot be overemphasized is role-playing. Practice, as they say, makes perfect. This is true in almost all realms. Your child may not need to practice their math facts like other children do, but they may need to practice their social skills. Parents can help by creating imaginary social scenarios that allow a child opportunity for dress rehearsal of behaviors. Most children find it very funny and helpful to exaggerate the wrong way to deal with an issue, as well. Other members of the family can get involved in the play, too, allowing everyone an opportunity to model how they would respond with guidance from the adults. Make sure you always end with a demonstration of a positive way to handle that situation.

⭐ Essential

Parents will be more successful at instituting role-playing if children are involved. You may choose to make a family jar of situations. As difficulties arise in your child's life, you and your child can write them down on slips of paper. Then, take turns acting out how to approach the event. Some examples might be finding someone to play with at recess, asking a girl on a date, speaking in an appropriate tone of voice to someone, etc.

Bullying

Gifted children over the years have relayed countless stories of the abuses they have suffered at the hands of those jealous or unsure of how to handle their abilities. Young children recount instances of forced isolation, punches, or items being thrown at them. High-school and middle-school aged children tell of the ridicule they were subjected to at the hands of others. Many were verbally or physically assaulted for breaking class curves or for being the "teacher's pet." Bullying can take on simple forms like calling someone names or tattling on them. It can also escalate to take on more egregious forms like physical assaults including pushing and tripping as well as emotional assaults such as spreading hateful rumors or painful exclusion.

Dr. Sylvia Rimm, noted psychologist and author specializing in gifted children, warns in a *Washington Post* article, "Some kids get away with it [being gifted] if they're really good at sports or very pretty. If kids are teased in the one area they have that's strong, there is this feeling of isolation and anger. Adults need to take it seriously because otherwise these kids go underground."

 Fact

According to a recent study in *Gifted Child Quarterly* quoted in the *Washington Post*, nearly two-thirds of eighth graders identified as academically gifted had suffered some form of bullying.

Part of the problem is the result of an oversensitized culture that fails to accurately articulate what bullying is. Bullying has been in the news frequently over the past few years, and the attitudes of teachers and administrators are changing and the tolerance level for bullying has markedly declined. However, teachers and administrators can become overwhelmed with investigating trivial instances and are often too overworked to address real bullying when it takes place. Make sure to talk to your child from a young age about what constitutes bullying. Making a list of true bullying situations may be a concrete way to help your child understand when to seek help from adults, versus handling the situation themselves. Be clear and provide age-appropriate examples so your child is not confused.

Well-meaning parents can also exacerbate the situation by telling their children that everyone gets teased, that they should stick up for themselves, or just to ignore the offending party. While these may be helpful adages in certain situations, they are not remedies for true bullying. Learning to deal with criticism and teasing may be a normal part of childhood, but dealing with physical, emotional, or sexual abuse is not. Children who are afraid to come forward may be forced to continue having interactions with the offender. Parents must make sure to listen to their children, and not dismiss what they are saying as "normal" childhood troubles. Gifted children may downplay the instances, so parents should also be alert to what they are not saying. Often, children have learned at an early age that their parents do not listen to or believe them when they try to talk to them, and may give up seeking help from their parents when they truly need it. They may also feel that they should be mature enough to handle it on their own. No one—no matter their age chronologically or intellectually—should suffer the burden of abuse alone or unaided. Gifted children need help from caring adults willing to ensure that such behaviors are stopped as well as punished.

 **Question**

What are the warning signs of bullying or abuse?
Parents should be on guard for warning signs that their gifted child is being bullied or abused. Normally happy children can become suddenly shy, afraid, or withdrawn. A child may demonstrate a seemingly irrational fear of attending school, feign headaches or sickness, or cry inconsolably. If your child demonstrates any of these symptoms, consider seeking professional help from your school or a local counselor.

Peer Pressure

All gifted children will face peer pressure of one type or another in their lifetime. In the elementary school years, most gifted children do not seem to face too many difficulties based on their high intelligence. Typical elementary school peer pressure takes the form of following fads, adopting particular mannerisms, and a desire to be like peers. Most peer pressure in the early years is internally driven by a desire to conform to the culture around. Parents should not worry too much about these issues, as this attempt to separate from parents and form an individual identity apart from one's parents (even one that is similar to peers) is natural and healthy. The best tactic is to remain supportive throughout your child's attempts to discover himself. Most of these forays into individuality at a young age are harmless and will provide wonderful stories in their adult years. While many attempts at discovering individual identity are both normal and healthy, any risky or illegal behaviors such as experimenting with drinking, drugs, or shoplifting are not to be excused, and should be promptly and strongly addressed by parents.

 **Essential**

Talk with your child from an early age about what makes a good friend. Discussing what good friends look and act like and pointing out examples helps reinforce how to build positive peer relationships later on for your child.

The elementary school years are also the time for parents to build a foundation of love and support for their child. In these relatively insignificant instances, you and your child will develop a pattern for dealing with peer pressure, conflicting desires, and power struggles that will have great bearing on all future communication. If you demonstrate to your child that you are not supportive of their growing need for independence or unwilling to compromise, they will most likely be unwilling to talk with you about changes and challenges in their adolescent years. Choose your battles carefully during these formative years. Try to take each situation as an individual learning and teaching opportunity to help build a caring relationship with your child, as well as to instill your own family's code of ethics and values. Taking the time to do this in the early years will pay dividends later on when the discussions are not on trivial subjects.

🅔 Alert

While parents should act as a firm foundation and supportive coach through these changes, make sure not to compromise your individual family values for the sake of your child's growing autonomy. Children thrive best in an environment of choice within limitations. Teach your child what is acceptable within your own family while at the same time finding a way for them to develop their own self.

The middle school and high school years are an altogether different matter. If parents have not built communication into their relationship prior to this point, it is next to impossible to do so at this juncture. You may well spend the next five to ten years having little to no idea what trials and challenges your child is facing at school with his peers. Most gifted middle-school and high-school children are facing the typical peer pressures of children this age. These include pressures to engage in risky behaviors (drinking, promiscuity, shoplifting, etc.). Gifted children also face an added element of peer pressure. Most gifted children sense that they are somehow different from their peers. Many face an added desire to belong or fit in to the social group. This can cause them to be more likely to participate in the risky behaviors previously mentioned, in hopes of fitting in and making friends. Gifted children may also be tempted to underachieve in order to find a place. They may try to "dumb down" their intelligence, or take school lightly.

As a parent, you can help your child in several ways. Listening to her feelings and providing a supportive sounding board can help tremendously. Many times, an empathetic adult can provide just enough comfort and guidance to help a teen fight against the desire to conform to the group. It might also benefit your child to participate in a variety of activities. In doing so, she may find a group where she fits just right without having to change who she is in order to fit.

🔵 Alert

Some children, particularly logical thinkers, appreciate the reminder that junior high and high school are a short and finite amount of time. Be careful, though, because other children—those more prone to emotionalism usually—may think that you are trivializing and belittling them with this information. Before employing this reasoning, make sure to evaluate which type of child you have on your hands.

At this point in development, most adolescents are past the point of looking at qualities that make up good friends. For most children, the desire to fit in and be liked is far more important than the qualities that make up a good friend. Many are willing to put up with being treating poorly if it means having a sense of belonging.

You are the most important factor in whether or not your child will succumb to peer pressure. Talking regularly and openly with your child from an early age will help build a relationship where they are willing to talk regularly and openly with you throughout their teenage years and into adulthood. Remember, gifted children know when they are being dismissed or condescended to. While they may not call you out on it, they will file it away in their memories and slowly withdraw from talking with you candidly and openly.

Depression

Depression is a very real and serious emotional disorder. It is diagnosed as a mental state marked by feelings of overwhelming sadness, a sense of worthlessness, and feelings of helplessness. Depression can have devastating effects on those that suffer from it as well as their families. While gifted children do not statistically have a higher rate of depression than their counterparts, many aspects of their giftedness can cause them to be sensitive to depressive episodes. Their giftedness can cause them to have a deep level of introspection and periods of excessive self-awareness. In addition, gifted children also have a high level of concern for social problems, often internalizing them. Gifted children are known for having "overexcitabilities" and intense sensitivities, causing them to respond more strongly to emotional stimuli and experiences. These factors can combine to lead to depression in the gifted. Gifted children often feel as though they need to solve their problems themselves, even from a young age, which can cause them to be less likely to seek help. Maintaining open dialogue with your child can help you to evaluate their emotional state and know when to seek help. It's important to emphasize that asking for help is not a sign of weakness and may help your child grow up into an adult unafraid to seek assistance when needed as well.

🅔❗ Alert

Recognizing the warning signs of depression early in your child can lead to treatment that saves their life. You should watch for fatigue and a decreased level of energy, a pervasive pessimism toward life, overeating or loss of appetite, feelings of guilt over things they can't control, or trouble concentrating and making decisions. If you see any combination of these signs in your child, seek help from a competent mental health care provider immediately.

Manipulation

Parents are also concerned about a gifted child's propensity for manipulation. They like to have things done a certain way—their way. Most gifted children (and gifted adults!) genuinely believe that their way is the best. However, they often resort to manipulation of others in order to get their way. Gifted kids have sophisticated conversational and debate skills; often, peers and adults may not even realize they have been manipulated till after the fact, if ever. They may also see lying, cheating, and exaggeration as tools to use to achieve their purpose rather than very wrong actions warranting serious punishment. It is very important that gifted children learn early that these actions will not be tolerated in your home. If you fail to catch them in a child's youth, they will become highly developed behaviors that are hard to catch and even harder to break.

Parents should have very clear rules for how to discuss concerns they may have. Gifted children can, and should, discuss how they are feeling and what they are thinking; however, they should do so in a healthy and respectful manner, just as adults. While your child may be an excellent arbitrator, they are still the child and you are the parent. Your decisions should be final, and your child should respect your authority. In your rules-and-consequences structure, you may build in a discussion time, but make sure that it is clear that while your child may offer their thoughts, the ultimate say is yours. In addition, the consequences of arguing or manipulation should be very clear. Make sure that you enforce those consequences every time; just one lapse becomes the time your child will remember in all future arguments—they're referred to as little lawyers for good reason! As much as possible, parents should try to speak as honestly with their children as possible to model appropriate communication strategies, so as not to negatively reinforce poor behaviors. Truthfully discuss your communication with your spouse or partner to evaluate whether you have been demonstrating any manipulation or dishonesty with your child or with others in front of your child. While instructing your child in right speech is important, modeling it with your actions is even more important.

How to Help

This chapter has identified many areas where gifted children can struggle regarding their social and emotional development as well as possibly strategies for parents to help their child with these areas. You can help your child by listening as they discuss their difficulties with social relationships. Provide support and advice when asked. Seize teachable moments to impart wisdom, and practice handling difficult situations with others.

Beyond those specific ways to help, the best help for your child is being involved in her life. Building a foundation of love and acceptance is the strongest tool you can give your child. Helping her develop an identity and a place within your family can provide her with a sense of self and assurance that will carry her through her developmental years and into adulthood.

CHAPTER 11

The Young and the Gifted

Most information on gifted children starts with school-age children. This can be frustrating for many parents of gifted children because they can sense that their child is different from a very early age. Parents want to know how to best help their very young gifted child, in order to give them the best possible start, even before they turn that magical age of five when kindergarten and most school programs begin.

Why It's Hard to Know

Most schools and programs will not test a child's intelligence until they are school age, and many intelligence and achievement tests are not eligible until children are eight years old, at least. This makes it difficult for a parent to determine if their preschooler is gifted or not. The reasons for this are complex. Historically, most schools did not offer services for gifted children until they were in second or third grade. Many in the gifted community also feel that simply knowing your child is gifted does not serve a purpose and that the true reason behind testing is to provide services or somehow better the life of the child being tested. Gifted tests are designed not to result in false positives (incorrectly identifying children as gifted who are not actually gifted). However, children who are tested too young may receive scores that are not indicative of their true ability. Many feel that the scores are not truly reflective of a child's intelligence until they are between seven and eight years old. The tests take time as well as concentration, which many young children are not capable of enduring.

Some schools are now beginning to offer services for children as early as kindergarten. Several tests have been designed or modified to accommodate young gifted children. Parents who would like to know whether or not their child is gifted for the purposes of enrolling in a program for gifted preschoolers may investigate some of these options. For others, the early behavior indicators may remain the most effective and best tool for determining whether or not your young child is gifted.

Early Signs of Giftedness

Parents can often tell that something is different about their child. However, most gifted advocates as well as resources begin providing information at the school-age level. There are some things that parents can watch for from birth through preschool that will help them identify giftedness early on.

Babies

For parents who know to recognize the signs, telltale signals of giftedness can be seen in babies. Gifted babies are very alert and watchful of what is going on around them, seeming to analyze people and their surroundings rather than merely looking at them. Gifted infants, like gifted children, seem to require less sleep than other infants. A gifted baby will need stimulation during the wakeful hours, seeming to be unsatisfied or demanding when they are not receiving attention or entertainment in some form. Additionally, gifted babies may be very sensitive to light, sound, and touch—early precursors for the overexcitabilities found in older gifted children. Gifted babies may show interest in books early by staring intently at the pictures or attempting to turn the pages.

They may also smile and laugh early, as well as mimicking facial expressions of those around them. Gifted babies may begin speaking earlier than normal, recognize letters and numbers as early as eighteen months, and begin reading as early as two years old. They may also be saying two-word phrases or uttering sentences as early as eleven months. These are just a few areas to watch for in your baby if you think he might be gifted.

 Alert

> The book *Boosting Your Baby's Brain Power* by Susan M. Heim and Holly Engel-Smothers has wonderful insight on how the baby's brain forms. The book also contains many fun and enriching activities to help foster intellectual development in babies from birth to one year.

Giving Your Baby a Boost

Parents can help develop their babies' intellectual skills in many ways. It is important to make sure your baby has a nutritious, well-balanced diet free from artificial and processed foods that inhibit proper brain growth. The first five years of life are very important, and your baby needs all the vitamins and nutrients from healthy fruits, vegetables, and other natural sources that he can get in order to ensure proper development. Young children also need good fats in their diet like those found in peanut butter (although parents should be careful to introduce nuts to their very young children in keeping with the recommendations of their pediatrician and other health care providers because of the prevalence of nut based allergies in contemporary society), olive oil, and real butter, as this helps to myelinate the neural pathways during brain development. It is important to make sure your child received enough proper nutrition to stimulate healthy brain development. Additionally, you are teaching healthy lifestyle choices that will carry your child through life. Parents can also start building communication skills from birth on. Talking to your baby, pausing to allow baby to respond, and then speaking again teaches early conversation skills in addition to helping your baby build his vocabulary.

Choosing developmentally appropriate, creative toys can foster your baby's brain development, as well. Avoid electronic toys that make noise and take the creativity out of your child's hands. Choose toys that can be used in multiple ways such as blocks or windup toys. These teach causal relationships, consequences, and beginning problem solving. Make sure that reading is a part of your young child's life by setting aside time to read to him at least once every day, although many times a day is preferable. Babies and toddlers love books with a singsong cadence, rhymes, bright colors, and large graphics. While you might be tempted to read your child the classics of your childhood, it is sometimes best to save those until your child is old enough to enjoy them and an early literacy foundation has already been built. Simple hand games also help develop early sequencing, memory, and patterning skills. They also help develop fine and gross motor skills for your child. Try peek-a-boo, patty cake, and others.

Most children do not require a substantial number of toys. In most instances, exposure to nature and interaction with adults and other children are more than sufficient for healthy child development. Many toys and products in the marketplace today are targeted at children but in actuality are detrimental to their intellectual as well as social and emotional growth and development. A good toy is one that can be used creatively in multiple ways to challenge your child's brain, that helps your child develop a new skill or enhance an existing skill, and will not go out of style in a short amount of time. It comes with few instructions, to allow your child freedom of experimentation. Toys that have complicated parts or will break easily should be avoided. Some toy awards to look for are The Oppenheim Award, The Parents' Choice Award, Dr. Toy's Best Children's Products, or The National Parenting Center's Seal of Approval.

✅ Fact

The American Academy of Pediatrics recommends that all children under age two refrain from watching television. Many studies have proven that watching television prior to age two can have harmful effects on brain development. This includes videos and television shows that are targeted at babies and young children. The information and images change rapidly, which confuses a young, growing brain, which can simply shut down when it encounters too much stimuli.

Toddlers and Preschoolers

As parents interact with their toddlers, more signs of giftedness can become evident. Gifted toddlers can follow directions as early as eighteen months. They can speak grammatically correct sentences by two years of age. Many gifted toddlers are actually late to begin speaking, but speak in complete sentences once they begin communicating. They memorize and recall facts easily as well as having extensive personal memories—sometimes to the frustration of their parents! Gifted toddlers are interested in puzzles very young and rapidly progress in the difficulty of puzzle solving. Preschoolers who are gifted are very curious and ask questions unceasingly, while rarely being satisfied with simple explanations. Oftentimes, they are fascinated by anything electronic, from calculators to computers. Many gifted toddlers and preschoolers have imaginary friends with whom they are involved in complex play scenarios. Gifted toddlers can begin learning to read by three years of age as well as do simple math calculations. One of the most enjoyable characteristics of young gifted children is their sense of humor and ability to tell as well as understand jokes. While this list in not complete, it does give parents some early indicators that their toddler or preschooler may be gifted.

🛑 Alert

It is helpful to note that gifted toddlers and preschoolers also learn the distinction between fantasy and reality from an early age. Many gifted children learn early on that Santa as well as the Tooth Fairy are not real. Some feel lied to or belittled when they come to this realization, while others carry on the charade because they sense that it is important to adults.

Giving Your Toddler a Head Start

Parents can start many different practices that will help their toddler to get ahead. Singing familiar children's songs as well as made up songs can help children to acquire new information. They can also teach motor skills, rhyme, rhythm, and other important skills. Toddlers can also learn from cleaning up after themselves. As early as nine- to twelve-month-old babies can benefit from being a part of routine household tasks like cleaning up. They teach children about order, categorization, shapes, and capacity—not to mention how to be a useful member of a community! Allowing your child to play in creative and messy ways fosters their growth, as well. Introducing unique and interesting foods can become a lesson in taking risks and dealing with new things. Children can also be exposed to new cultures and traditions. Using positive and reality-based discipline is helpful in development maturity, as well. Young children learn cause-and-effect relationships, problem solving, conflict resolution, and self-control as you discipline them and show them that actions have corresponding reactions and consequences.

Why Start Early

Gifted preschoolers present a particularly challenging dilemma. If there are few teachers in the school setting trained to identify and teach gifted children, there are dramatically fewer prepared to handle a gifted preschooler. Gifted preschoolers may be amongst the most underserved in the gifted population.

Historically, this has not been as much of a problem, as most children were educated at home until they reached school age. Preschool-aged children were either given appropriately challenging activities at home or were given the freedom to create their own intellectually stimulating pursuits. As more and more children enter school settings at an earlier age, gifted children have more of a problem. They are required to conform to societal and educational expectations from a much younger age.

In gifted girls, this can lead to learning to please the teacher and appear less intellectually gifted from an earlier age. By the time a gifted preschooler reaches elementary school, she may have sufficiently conformed to the point of forgetting how bright she truly is in her attempt to maintain the status quo to make the teacher happy.

For gifted preschool boys, this can become even more devastating. Preschool-age boys who are not challenged do not become teacher pleasers; they become problem children in their attempts to gain mental stimulation in whatever way they can. Gifted boys also have more difficulty reining in their excessive kinetic energy, which makes the amount of sedentary activity common to the classroom an insurmountable hurdle. Gifted preschool boys are often labeled as troublemakers from the onset, which becomes a label they internalize and carry with them. They also begin to form negative feelings about the school setting in general, as they routinely get into trouble and fail to be challenged. By the time they enter the traditional school setting for kindergarten, they have already decided that school is not the place for them to learn.

Unfortunately, highly gifted children (those in the 95th percentile) only occur in approximately 1 out of 1,000 preschoolers, and profoundly gifted children (those in the 99.9th percentile) are as rare as 1 in 10,000 preschoolers. Most preschool teachers will rarely if ever see gifted children of this nature. It is hard to convince preschools to invest in training and resources for the young and gifted when the odds are so low. Preschools, like many other academic institutions, assume that these children will do just fine in the traditional setting, and fail to prepare for or invest in the necessary training and supplies to adequately challenge them when they are presented.

It is important for parents to be aware of these realities when choosing a preschool. If you know or suspect your child is gifted, be prepared to ask questions about how a preschool challenges bright children. In addition, your need to advocate for your child may begin early, as you seek to work with the preschool you choose to provide necessary stimulation your child needs, which may come in a variety of forms both academic as well as allowing your child the traditional preschool experiences of outside play and finger painting.

How to Challenge Your Young Gifted Child

Parents who are looking to challenge their child at home or as an enhancement to a preschool curriculum have many options. Gifted children love learning about new topics. Encourage their intellectual curiosity by helping them research the topics they are interested in. Work together to present the information by making posters, writing their own books, and creating PowerPoint presentations to show relatives and friends. Young children love visiting the library, receiving their first library card, and choosing their own books. Don't limit your child to the youth section of the library; many gifted children thoroughly enjoy the nonfiction section as you work together to choose appropriate selections within their fields of interest. Keep in mind, also, that most contemporary literature is written at an eighth-grade reading level, which most gifted children arrive at by middle elementary school. If your child enjoys fiction, encourage them to read classical literature, or pieces written by authors you know to be more challenging than the mainstream texts may be.

Provide enriching learning opportunities for your young child. You can do this by taking them to museums or on field trips to places they might find interesting. As you begin investigating your local community, you will find countless opportunities for academic enrichment you can share with your child. Many parks and recreation groups host classes that can be enriching for a young child, even if they are not academically challenging.

Essential

Some parents might consider asking for a museum membership for a child's birthday or special holiday celebration. While toys can break or become easily mastered, a membership to the zoo or local children's museum can be enjoyed over and over again, providing a wonderful and enriching experience for your child.

Gifted toddlers and preschoolers also enjoy experimenting with art and music. Take your child to art exhibits, and then find ways for them to experiment in these art mediums on their own at home. Try introducing your child to an instrument such as the piano. They may also enjoy listening to the works of great composers.

Parents might consider forming an enrichment club, taking turns planning science experiments, or visiting different parents' work locations.

Alert

Parents need to be sensitive to their own child. Make sure that you have an understanding of your child's strengths and weaknesses in addition to their intellectual needs. In providing enrichment and challenges for your child, always be aware that what you are asking is appropriate to their abilities. Be careful that you are not pushing your child beyond what they are capable of but are helping them achieve their full potential.

What to Look for in a Preschool

Choosing the right preschool can be just as difficult as choosing an elementary, middle, or high school for your gifted child. It helps to know what you are looking for in a school. More than any other schools, preschools tend to fall into two primary categories: developmental or academic.

A Developmental Preschool

A developmental preschool will focus primarily on the physical, social, and emotional skills your child needs to be successful in their later schooling. A developmental preschool might have a variety of types of activities. They may have a pretend play area where children practice social interactions and pretend play. Additionally, they may do arts and crafts to help children learn to hold a pencil, cut with scissors, and glue items. These activities help develop fine-motor skills. Parents may also find lots of singing and playing to help children with their gross-motor skills. These are some of the learning disciplines common at a developmental preschool.

Academic Preschools

At an academic preschool, children may have entrance requirements such as knowing their alphabet or being able to hold a pencil correctly. Many academic preschools focus on teaching young children to read and write, do early math computations, and other skills. The emphasis is more on the child's intellectual development, with less focus on the social- and physical-skills development. These schools tend to be very good for children who have learned their letters early or are very inquisitive and driven to acquire knowledge.

Montessori Preschools

Montessori preschools are an altogether separate type of preschool from the traditional developmental or academic preschool.

Montessori schools are typically run by teachers and administrators who have had specific Montessori training. Montessori preschools focus on allowing children to choose from a variety of activities, all designed to be developmentally appropriate and challenging. Many gifted children enjoy a Montessori environment that allows freedom of choice as well as multisensory learning opportunities. Other gifted children can become frustrated by the lack of structure and the limited ability for cognitive development. When making your preschool decision, it might be worth visiting a Montessori preschool in order to evaluate all of your options to find the best fit for your child.

 Fact

Montessori schools are named for the pioneering work of Maria Montessori, a doctor in the early 1900s in Italy who observed children at play and developed a system for teaching them based on a "prepared environment" that held all the resources from which children could learn life skills.

Which type of preschool really depends on you and your child. Some gifted children benefit from attending a developmental preschool where they learn social skills and gain important developmental practice in many areas where they may be weaker because of their asynchronous development. Other gifted children can become bored and frustrated in a developmental preschool setting where they are not academically challenged.

Gifted preschoolers can thrive in an academic setting where they are exposed to exciting new mental challenges, given early access to learning to read and do mathematics, and interact with like-minded friends. On very rare occasions, a parent can find a preschool that addresses both their child's academic as well as developmental needs. As a parent, you will have to decide which area it is most important for a school to address. You may choose to send your child to a school that focuses on the areas where she is resistant to your help in teaching her. Parents who choose either school need to make sure to address the other areas at home in order to ensure that their preschooler is well rounded and as best prepared for elementary school as possible.

Remember to start looking early, as most preschools have waiting lists for availability. It's never too early to begin to tour schools, speak with other parents, and start making decisions.

CHAPTER 12

Gifted Girls

When discussing the development and care of gifted children, it is important to note that boys and girls report vastly different experiences of growing up gifted. There are many unique characteristics of and challenges to being gifted for girls than there are for boys, like the differences in the ways that girls' brain process information in addition to how they learn. This includes some myths and stereotypes as well as simple differences in gender such as what subjects girls are better at or what makes for the best career path for a young woman. Parents who have gifted girls face a different set of experiences than parents of boys do. It is important for parents to be aware of these differences, as well as be prepared to address them as they present themselves throughout their daughter's development.

How Giftedness Is Different in Girls

Giftedness, on the whole, has traditionally been more valued and supported in males than in females. Parents are far more likely to believe that their son is gifted and request testing than they are to request testing for their daughter. While more and more girls are being accepted into gifted programs, the stereotypes continue to persist. In elementary school, the number of children being accepted to and participating in gifted programs is about equal.

However, in middle school and high school, these numbers shift to represent far more males than females in gifted and advanced-placement courses. By adulthood, the numbers are no longer comparable.

Being a gifted female is a special experience with twists and turns along the way. There are several common transitions most gifted women share in.

Childhood

For many gifted women, childhood is an idyllic period. The world is filled with wonder and excitement, new mysteries waiting to be explored. The very lucky gifted young girl has a supportive family and lives in an environment that encourages her creative and intellectual pursuits.

Most gifted girls remember their early childhood fondly for the joy of freedom and the passion of new daily discoveries.

Prior to elementary school, gifted girls speak, read, write, and pass through most of life's developmental markers faster than their gifted male counterparts.

As they pass out of early childhood and into the school-age years, life begins to become more troublesome for gifted girls. Upon entering school, they learn that they are not like everyone else. In addition, their gifts and abilities are not always appreciated. Most girls learn very early that behaving according to social norms makes everyone happier and causes adults to like them. Gifted girls are very intuitive, and learn these social rules quickly. They begin to play down their intelligence for the sake of making teachers and peers happy. Outwardly, their demeanor may not change as they shift their focus from being good at school and enjoying academic challenges to being popular and having lots of friends. It is important to teach your daughter that these two goals do not have to be mutually exclusive. You can help her find friends who are also smart and talented, teaching her that true friends can be smart, but do not base their affections solely on her intelligence.

Unfortunately, this also coincides with the most common time-frame for gifted testing. Most gifted placement occurs around third grade. By this time, many gifted girls have learned to downplay or second guess their abilities. During testing, they are afraid to disappoint others or make mistakes that diminish their scores and their resulting IQ test ratings.

For some reason, the myth persists that it is good for boys to appear smart, but better for girls to fit in with others. Girls pick up on this message whether it is verbally spoken or not.

ⓔ✪ Essential

It is important for parents of gifted girls to help them maintain a positive self-image. Make sure that you are giving your daughter the counter-cultural message that it is okay for her to be smart and that it is most important for her to be true to herself. You can do this by encouraging your daughter's interests. Support her in her creative and academic pursuits to allow her to fully develop her passions and abilities.

Adolescence

In adolescence, the intensity and pressures that began in elementary school intensify. Biologically, girls are facing the drive to develop independence and separate from their family. Added to this are societal pressures to be pretty, be popular, and fit in. In the early teenage years, gifted girls are likely to hide their academic abilities in order to be more like the other girls around them. Friends and a place in your school's social order are very important, and oftentimes trump making good grades or ensuring that your daughter is challenged academically.

Fact

Middle school is the make-it-or-break-it time for most gifted girls. During these few years, most girls will make a decision to either maintain their intellectual standing or to fit in with their peers. Parents need to recognize the significance of these changes and the impact their daughter's decisions will have on the rest of her academic learning.

Some school districts are starting to recognize the impact this is having on the education of girls. Several are responding by offering single-gender programming. Many girls, and boys, can find great comfort and belonging in a program such as this. You may consider investigating to see if a girls-only school might be a good fit for your daughter.

Alert

In the adolescent years, many girls may want to attend a certain school or be a part of a specific program. Some may have good reasons for their choice while others may base the decision on more superficial reasons. As a parent, remember that the final say on school choices is up to you. While you may choose to allow your daughter to express her opinion on the matter, the decision should be made by her parents.

Adulthood

Parents are fond of reminding their children that childhood is only temporary. While this often provides little solace to the child, the words are very true. Perhaps they are most true for gifted girls. It is important for gifted girls to know that there is life after middle school and high school. Some day, they will attend college, begin careers, and venture out into the world. While the world may not be as progressive as parents and advocates for the gifted would like it to be, it is certainly much more accepting of gifted young women than most high school campuses are.

Gifted girls can experience a renewed sense of freedom and belonging as they reach higher education.

Unique Challenges for Girls

Gifted girls in particular face challenges as they grow up. Many of the behaviors that are characteristics of being gifted are encouraged in boys while chastised in girls. Calling out answers, holding dogmatically to a viewpoint, and asking lots of questions are examples of behaviors that are considered acceptable for gifted boys but rude for gifted girls. Girls carry a heavier expectation of compliance and conformity.

Girls are particularly susceptible to the desire to fit in. Many girls are willing to sabotage their passions and their learning for the sake of fitting in with their peers. Some of this is rooted in a compassionate nature—not wanting others to feel badly by standing out or being better at something than they are. Additionally, gifted girls may also play down their intelligence, acting as though they worked hard or got lucky instead of accepting that they are intelligent. For girls, the pressure not to call undue attention to oneself is tremendous.

 Alert

Many girls are successful at managing to fit in; however, later on they describe an intense loneliness as the cost. By altering her personality to make friends, she forces herself to travel through life feeling like an imposter waiting to be found out. Be sensitive to the fact that your daughter may be feeling this way and look for opportunities to talk through these feelings.

The Math-Science Myth

It has been a long-held belief that boys are better than girls at math. Many accept this stereotype to be true even amongst gifted children. Several studies have been done to investigate this myth. Up until age fourteen, girls tend to outscore boys on most achievement-based tests in almost all subject areas. However, what is also true is that girls stop participating in advanced classes in high school, especially math- and science-related courses. Studies have shown that gifted girls underestimate their abilities while gifted boys overestimate their own skills. This allows gifted boys the confidence to take higher-level courses that many girls resist for fear of failure. They are not underperforming in math and science; girls are simply underperforming in these areas as well as others. Girls are more likely to take a less challenging class that they think they will be successful in rather than a difficult course where they might struggle or fail.

While gifted girls may be just as good as boys at math and science, they may also be just as susceptible to another gifted phenomena. Most gifted children become accustomed to understanding new concepts quickly and easily in their early school years. They begin to expect that everything will come easily to them with little effort or practice. Unfortunately, this is not true. Everyone reaches a point in their academic career where learning takes more work on the part of the student—for some it may be in calculus class while for others it may happen balancing chemical equations. Gifted boys are more likely to push through this stumbling block while gifted girls will drop out of a course when it proves challenging. You can help your child through this by making sure she is faced with challenges from a young age. Learning to work hard, fail, and try again are important life skills that gifted children sometimes have difficulty developing because of their breadth of abilities. These coping skills will carry them through many of life's troubles to make them well-rounded problem solvers and risk takers.

Thankfully, these gaps appear to be decreasing some over time, as the number of girls who are enrolling in higher-level mathematics and science courses is increasing. Many programs have been created in the last two decades to help foster the self-confidence of girls. Girls have a growing number of examples of successful women in traditionally male professions. As more role models are available, along with better access to classes and programs, girls are more likely to envision themselves succeeding in these areas. Parents and gifted professionals can also continue to encourage and advocate for gifted girls in the mathematics and science fields.

Helping Gifted Girls Succeed

Dr. Sylvia Rimm, a researcher and counselor who works with gifted children in her private practice, shares many useful strategies for helping your gifted daughter to succeed. She suggests making sure to be an advocate for your daughter without being a judge. That means encouraging and praising your daughter while recognizing that she receives plenty of judgment already from her peers, teachers, and herself. You can also help your daughter succeed by teaching her the value of competition. A healthy appreciation for the benefits of competing and winning can help your daughter face challenges of life with a positive attitude and determination to be successful. Don't alter your expectations because you have a daughter. Continue to expect accomplishments as great from your daughter as you would from a son. Consider traveling abroad with your daughter to expose her to other cultures and a world bigger than the one found in her high school. You can foster this sense of a larger world than her peer group by helping her become involved in volunteer and charitable works in your community and beyond. Help her to choose a project she feels passionate about to design and gain the support of others. Many gifted girls also enjoy becoming involved in groups that are specifically for girls, such as Girl Scouts or Girls State program where they can meet other strong, independent, and talented young women. If you do not have programs like these in your area, find biographies of successful women to read with your daughter.

 **Essential**

You might consider joining together with other mothers of gifted girls to create your own gifted girls club. Get together weekly or monthly to share experiences of being a gifted girl. Invite guest speakers from the community to share their experiences as children and as adults. Creating an open forum for discussion as well as examples of how bright the future can be will help your gifted girl see that there is more to life than what she might be experiencing right now.

One of the most important reminders is that your daughter may not fit in socially, and that is okay. Try not to pressure her to make friends or to fit in with her peers. Fitting in may mean compromising who she is or giving up on her special gifts. Sometimes the price a gifted girl must make to be true to herself is in forsaking certain friends and social standing. Build a strong foundation in who she is at home as an important member of your family and her community to help offset any sense of feeling alone she might have in her school experience. Continue to do this by being a positive example for your daughter as a mother by setting high standards for yourself, without compromising to meet the expectations of society.

Alert

A great resource for parents of gifted girls is *See Jane Win* by Sylvia Rimm. This book is intended to be read with your daughter, or you can give it to your daughter to read. She will love the practical advice and the straightforward writing style, which will help her feel as though the author is talking right to her, encouraging her to succeed in life.

The Future Is Bright for Gifted Girls

Compared to history, gifted young women today have more options than ever. Consider some interesting statistics. According to the Department of Public Employees, in 2010 women had made some surprising advances over previous decades.

- Women have gone from representing 5.1 million workers in the 1900s to representing over 66 million in 2009, which is roughly 46 percent of the labor force.
- Women are projected to make up 78 billion members of the workforce by 2018.
- In addition, 73 percent of those working women hold white collar jobs as opposed to jobs in service or trade-related industries.
- Women continue to earn more bachelor's degrees than men, and earn around 59 percent of all postsecondary degrees (this includes 53 percent of doctoral degrees, 49 percent of medical degrees, as well as 44 percent of all law degrees among other high-level professional fields).

While this may seem like a jumble of numbers and statistics, it means something to gifted women. Women are surviving the adolescent years and going on to college and postsecondary success. Where in previous years women were more likely to be in blue collar or support roles in the community, they are now becoming active and thriving members of some of the highest roles in society. These numbers signal opportunity. Opportunity for your gifted daughter to do anything or become anything that she dreams of being. She no longer has to choose from teacher, nurse, or librarian. As you talk with her about her hopes and dreams, the world is full of limitless possibilities for her to choose from for her future.

 **Essential**

While the statistics and facts regarding the development of gifted young girls can seem bleak and disheartening at times, many gifted girls travel through these troublesome years relatively unscathed. Armed with knowledge and supportive strategies, you can help your daughter become a success story instead of a statistic. Provide her with positive examples, your caring support, and limitless love to make sure that she becomes everything her gifts and talents can help her to be.

CHAPTER 13

Gifted Boys

Just as there are certain unique facets of giftedness related to being a girl, there are also many special considerations that relate to being a boy as well as being gifted. Boys face an entirely different set of stereotypes and considerations that need to be examined to fully understand the experience of being gifted as a young man. As a parent to a young man in modern society, it is important to be aware of current research on gender differences in brain development. Parents should also be prepared to address some of the unique learning styles of boys in order to ensure their academic needs are being met in their school setting. These are a few of the issues evaluated here in order to help parents of young men.

How Giftedness Is Different for Boys

Most parents would readily concede that boys and girls are different. No matter how schools and families try to socialize them in the same way, you can't change the fact that there are inherent variations between males and females. This is true even in the ways that their brains function, especially relating to their giftedness.

While there is no difference in the actual level of intelligence capable between men and women, scientists have found compelling research that suggests that men and women actually have tremendously varied brains. Boys have more gray matter in their brains while girls have more white matter. Gray matter is responsible for processing information in the brain while white matter controls the connections made regarding information. Simply put, men are better at analyzing information while women are more suited to drawing inference and making parallels.

Additionally, scientists have determined that boys tend to perform better at specialized tasks as well as tasks involving spatial awareness. Girls perform better on language development and emotional intelligence. Unfortunately for boys, schools are very language based, which is why the gender gap in education persists. Added to that is the fact that most teachers are females, who tend to teach (often unintentionally) to the learning styles of girls because that is the more comfortable teaching method for them.

Fact

A recent study done by Thomas S. Dee from Swarthmore College, quoted in the *Washington Post*, found that the previously existing gender gap in reading performance between boys and girls could be reduced to nearly a third of what it was by having boys spend one year of English instruction with a male teacher.

Other distinctions between the ways that boys and girls learn may surprise you. As early as kindergarten, girls have developed faster processing skills, allowing them to score higher on timed tests and activities. Boys have a slower processing speed, which is better suited for problem-solving tasks as well as those that require more in-depth thinking as opposed to on-the-spot answers. You can also see this in the gender gap when it comes to reading fluency scores. In elementary and middle school, part of a student's reading ability is measured by how fluidly they read. A boy's slower processing speed may inhibit his ability to read aloud in these situations. This is something for parents to be aware of, as many young boys do not like reading aloud in class or at home for precisely this reason.

 Alert

> To get around these difficulties with processing speed and fluency, parents can ask for an alternate option. Parents might suggest that the teacher give their son a passage to read silently in a given time, then have him answer questions and respond. This is a variation that would allow for the boy to show his comprehension and reading abilities without being hampered by his slower processing skills.

Boys additionally process information better auditorily, through hearing. Girls tend to process information better through visual means. This is important in the classroom and at home because it determines how boys will be most successful. Your son may prefer listening to a book on tape with you while your daughter may prefer reading it alongside you. In the classroom, your son may do better when given a verbal spelling quiz while your daughter may prefer a written exam. This research and other studies are being used by educators to determine if boys and girls would perform better in single-gender settings, where instruction can be geared toward the strengths of each. If your son is struggling in a traditional classroom setting, you might consider investigating these learning differences further to suggest to his teacher or implement at home.

Gifted Boys Throughout Their Lifetime

Your son will not stop being gifted once he finishes school. His giftedness will follow him throughout his life, changing and growing as he does. As a parent, it will be exciting for you to share in his experiences as he matures and learns.

Childhood

In childhood, there are several factors specific to gifted boys. Preschool and elementary school boys struggle to find a place in a traditionally female-dominated environment. Most teachers are women and instruction tends to be geared toward learning strategies that are commonly successful with girls. Boys need an environment with physical involvement, hands-on activities, and a fast pace. This can be difficult for them to find in a traditional school setting. Young boys trying to learn can be seen as discipline problems because in their zeal they may yell answers in classroom settings, leave their seat, or behave erratically from excitement.

Most boys are gifted in either logical-mathematical or spatial areas, whereas most girls are gifted in verbal areas. Schools tend to be geared toward more verbal activities and assessments, which leave gifted boys out in terms of having their need to be challenged met. This gender stereotype is also part of the reason why many boys develop an aversion to school and learning, feeling that it is boring and just not for them.

By later elementary school, boys have often learned what kind of behavior is acceptable in school. While their excitement at learning in the school environment has diminished, most boys learn to demonstrate socially acceptable behaviors of acting tough, staying out of trouble, avoiding questions, and suppressing their emotions. Many begin to use their intelligence to be funny or act like a class clown. They may also make sure that their academic successes are balanced out by more seemingly masculine successes in areas like sports.

Adolescence

Adolescence typically takes one of two turns for a gifted young man. On the one hand, it can become acceptable for boys to be seen as intelligent. Society in general seems to favor intelligence in young men once they reach the point of adolescence. Boys are more likely than girls to be called on to volunteer in class. They are also more likely to be given leadership positions within the classroom and school setting. In adolescence, academic opportunities become more diversified, allowing gifted boys to take more classes geared toward their specific interests. Additionally, they are exposed to more males as teachers and authority figures, which can provide more positive role models than they have found before. Boys also have access to a greater variety of sports, both team and individual, to participate in along with many art, theater, and other outside opportunities to meet their diverse interests.

Alert

Interestingly, studies have shown that most boys more readily accept a talent in a sport as being gifted than to accept that some children are gifted academically.

On the other hand, some gifted boys may face pressure either internally or externally to play down their smarts. Some boys feel as though it is not fair in a way for them to be so smart, so they can try to level the playing field by holding back their knowledge. They may try to help a friend share an answer or deflect attention for being intelligent, feeling that if everyone appears to have equal intelligence that is fairer.

Additionally, boys in their early teen years are also keen to fit in. Sometimes, athletics and extracurricular activities take precedence over academic pursuits when it comes to fitting in and building a social group. Socially, a boy who is smart is more likely to be accepted for his intelligence if he is also athletic. A boy who is not athletic may face stereotypes of being a nerd or other negative connotations.

Fact

A recent study determined that 90 percent of extreme underachievers in school are boys. This is important to the discussion on gifted boys, because for some reason boys persist in being underachievers at a far greater rate than young women. Parents of boys need to be particularly on guard against underachievement, watching for early warning signs in elementary school before its damages become irreversible in middle and high school.

In athletics, boys find an outlet for the strong competitive drive that is a biological force not only as a male but also as a gifted child. In most classrooms today, competition is minimized in an attempt to level the playing field and build self-esteem for all students. This is particularly detrimental to the gifted boy who is internally driven to compete with others and with himself. Removing this component of the academic environment takes some of the fun out of learning for him. He may then funnel that competitive drive into a sport or other activity. Parents can help by making schoolwork competitive at home, in a positive and healthy way. Set individual goals for him based on past performances. In doing so, you will return some of the challenge back to his schooling and hopefully help engage him more.

Adulthood

The future gets brighter for males. Studies have found that men are more adept at assessing their own intelligence than women. A *Time* magazine article called this "the hubris of men and humility of women effect." Women are more likely to downplay or underestimate their own intelligence while men are more able to accurately assess or even overestimate their own intelligence. Researchers also found that both men and women believe men to be smarter overall than women, regardless of the scientific evidence that both genders are equally intelligent based on IQ scores.

This works out in men's favor because it instills them with confidence and boldness. Men who know that they are intelligent are more aggressive in applying for positions, speaking out about their strengths, and overcoming their difficulties.

A gifted young man who perseveres through the trials and tribulations of school and adolescence has a bright future full of exciting opportunities for him to use his intelligence and talents to be a success.

Special Challenges for Gifted Boys

Boys face many special challenges, not the least of which is underachievement. Beginning in late elementary school, many gifted boys begin to underachieve. They refuse to do homework, won't participate in certain tasks, or withdraw from previously enjoyed academic activities. The reasons for this are varied. Some boys may begin to be teased for being smart around this age. Being smart may take on a feminine connotation from which a young boy may try to separate himself. Boys may simply want to exert their independence and rebel against authority figures. Regardless of the reason, failure to achieve in school becomes a real challenge for gifted boys.

Gifted boys in childhood have another challenge. Gifted children are emotionally intense. They experience things more deeply and more profoundly. These feelings need to find a safe outlet. Most boys learn from a young age that feelings are bad and not to be expressed or talked about. A young gifted boy needs to have at least one strong parent relationship where he can learn to talk through and express the strong emotions he is dealing with. Without this supportive connection with a caregiver, a young boy learns to bottle his feelings and to fear sharing them. This can have disastrous results in his later life and social interactions.

Finally, gifted boys face the challenge of finding a place as a male in a complex society. Boys learn that certain behaviors are considered classically male. These include engaging in daring or risky behaviors and acting macho, hiding your emotions, refusing help from others, and the need to dominate or maintain a position of authority. These masculine behaviors can lead a young gifted man to be conflicted. These are isolating behaviors at a time when a young man is in need of support, encouragement, and guidance. The challenge is for parents to help fight against these stereotypes in order to help their gifted boy become successful.

The ADHD Controversy

Many people don't realize how similar the characteristics are between giftedness and Attention Deficit/Hyperactivity Disorder (ADHD). Boys are quick to be diagnosed with or accused of having ADHD. The speed with which they are identified as gifted is not nearly so rapid. When you look at the following characteristics, what comes to mind?

- Fidgets
- Has difficulty maintaining eye contact
- Shifts from side to side while speaking
- Forgetful
- Daydreams
- Careless with work
- Lack of interest in details
- Stubborn

Upon first glance, this might seem like a behavioral diagnosis list for ADD or ADHD. However, it is actually a list of behaviors commonly found amongst the gifted.

You can see from looking at these characteristics why so many young boys are being labeled as having poor attention skills. Let's be honest: It is much easier to medicate a child than it is to investigate a little further. It is certainly much more difficult to make sure that they are being academically stimulated on a regular basis. While most teachers are well meaning, often a diagnosis of ADHD means missing out on the opportunity to challenge some of the best and brightest young male minds.

 Fact

Many people are under the mistaken assumption that ADHD only affects boys. It is true that it seems to be more prevalent and more diagnosed in young men; however, girls can also be diagnosed with ADHD. Girls manifest the symptoms in different ways, most specifically with the absence of physical aggression that can be a factor for many young boys.

If someone is trying to diagnose your child as ADHD, make sure that you also request that he is tested for a gifted program. Often, a very bright student may exhibit the symptoms of ADHD when he is bored or not being stimulated enough intellectually in his current environment.

Why Gifted Boys Just Won't Sit Still!

Gifted children experience life differently from other children. It is almost as if they are viewing life in high definition. This affects many areas of their life, and the most compelling may be with regard to their high levels of energy.

Gifted children have long been said to need less restoring time than other children. They sleep fewer hours than other infants, stop taking naps sooner, and sleep less once they give up naps. By elementary school, while most children are still requiring ten to twelve hours of sleep, a gifted child may do just fine with seven to eight hours of sleep, rising early and staying up late with seemingly endless energy in between. In addition, they seem to generate and radiate energy. This is particularly true for gifted boys. Even at times when a young boy should be sitting, such as when concentrating on a hobby or watching television, he may be moving from side to side. While talking, he may sway or attempt to twist or walk in place. He might prefer to run from place to place rather than walking. When working at a project, he might jump out of his seat for no apparent reason to run to the other side of the room. This is very normal and to be expected from your gifted child. However, this is another instance where gifted boys can be misunderstood. These behaviors are particularly difficult in social settings such as school and church, where it is important for your child to learn to manage his excess energies.

 **Essential**

Explaining ahead of time what is going to happen, the expected behaviors, and the reasons behind them can help a child be successful. For example, on a trip planned to the museum, parents can explain beforehand that certain behaviors will help them get the most out of the experience. Museum rules dictate a quiet voice and no running. Let your child know that if he is feeling extra energy, appropriate outlets would be walking to the water fountain to get a drink or asking to take a break to go outside. Make sure to take plenty of breaks as needed to ensure a fun outing for everyone participating.

Parents can try a few simple practices to help a young boy manage his extra energy. They can start by making sure that their son gets enough physical activity prior to any time he will need to sit still. Arrive at church early so he has some time to run and play before being expected to sit down for the service. Make sure he gets to school early enough to participate in before-school recess time. Another strategy that often works is teaching a small, unnoticeable movement. Many little boys learn to twiddle their thumbs or roll a small ball around in their hand. Having some small action to use up some excess kinetic energy frees their mind and the rest of their body to be more successful at focusing. Many children benefit from chewing gum, perhaps one of the best and easiest tactics as long as your child knows how to properly dispose of the gum when he is finished.

More often than not, children with lots of excess energy learn to be successful. Young boys can become good at physically demanding sports. They can also develop skills for specific tasks such as building, artwork, or science. Tasks that take more specific, concentrated energy seem to take more energy and help their focus.

Take heart if you have a particularly rambunctious child. While few boys outgrow this symptom of giftedness, most learn to harness it and use it to their advantage. It seems as though they can manage to accomplish more in each day because of the extra energy they have to apply to the tasks at hand. This causes them to become great leaders and successful in many of their endeavors while still having the energy to lead a productive and well-rounded life.

Helping Gifted Boys Succeed

The key to helping gifted boys succeed is three-fold: help them find their passion, free them to be emotionally expressive, and allow them to celebrate their intelligence.

First, parents can build a foundation where knowledge is celebrated, not diminished. From early childhood, help your son see that being smart is a positive trait that can lead to many future successes. Help build his confidence in his intellectual abilities by providing a supportive foundation when, socially, his confidence in the importance of his intelligence may be in danger. Continue to reinforce this with your own life experiences as well as examples in books and the lives of people who became successful because of their academic abilities.

Next, you can help your son by teaching him to express himself emotionally. Bottling up emotions and being unable to deal with them may be one of the primary causes for lack of achievement in young men. Helping your son feel free to express himself and to seek outside counsel and support will give him skills for life. It is especially important that boys feel as though they can talk to their fathers about the way that they may be feeling or how their experiences are affecting them. Dads can help by volunteering stories from their growing up years and by providing an open-ended communication style that allows their son to feel free to come to them to talk.

Essential

Parents should remember that boys are especially in need of positive verbal reinforcement. Many parents have little trouble finding ways to praise their daughters, but boys seem to receive this type of verbal reinforcement less frequently. Sometimes fathers fear making their sons overly emotional or "soft," but the reality is that many young boys are emotionally insecure and in desperate need of kind words and gentle encouragements.

Finally, help your son find what he feels passionate about in life. Passion is what drives young men to greatness. Many boys without a burning desire toward a goal or accomplishment simply become apathetic. Without something driving your son on to a higher purpose, he will most likely become another underachieving statistic. All children have passions, and as a parent, you can work to find and cultivate those interests. They may change and develop as your child matures, but you can start nurturing them from a young age so that your son knows you are supportive of his goals and interests.

Read the biographies of great men from history, visit museums, and find mentors within your community who can provide positive examples and access to information as well as experience.

CHAPTER 14

Relationships and the Gifted Child

Gifted parents want their child to have a positive relationship with them and others, but this is a struggle for many gifted children. For whatever reason, gifted children tend to have difficulty forming relationships and handling social situations. Many experience difficulties in these areas early on in life, and decide that solitary play is easier and more enjoyable. There are some steps parents can take to help their children build positive relationships.

Helping Your Child Communicate

Effective communication, a key to most relationships, is an area where gifted children particularly struggle. Oftentimes, they can tell that something is not working but are unable to pinpoint and correct their missteps. Other times, a child may be completely unaware of how others perceive his communication style. Either way, parents can work together with their child to help him learn positive communication practices.

Communicating with Parents

The relationship between a parent and child is a complicated one. Parents want to be involved in their child's life, but the older children get the more space and independence they desire. In their attempt to build a communicative relationship, parents can try too hard. As a parent, make sure that you are reading your child's signals. If your child starts to withdraw from you, you may be pushing too hard. With young children, asking questions can be a helpful practice. Try to ask open-ended questions that require more than a one-word answer. How and why questions are better conversation starters than others might be. Parents should also keep in mind that kids can tell when you are simply probing for information. Often, the most innocent questions can be misconstrued. Though it is difficult to build these skills, it is worth the result that will come with time and patience.

 **Essential**

> One avenue to start building healthy communication practices can start when your child begins attending school. If possible, query your child as soon as she arrives home from school, ask her what the best and worst parts of her day were. Acknowledging the difficult parts of the day but keeping the focus on the good parts of the day helps her frame her day in a positive light without minimizing her troubles.

Remember that the older your child gets, especially approaching adulthood, the more your relationship matures as well. With the rights that come along with maturity, come responsibilities, and one of those responsibilities is voluntary communication. Growing up is a gradual process, as is your parental relinquishment of total control. As you ask questions of your older gifted child, make sure that you don't sound like a police officer interrogating a witness. Adolescents can be defensive of their growing need for autonomy and may withdraw if they feel their independence is being threatened. If you continue to push, you will create a downward spiral that will lead to parent and child constantly being at odds.

Gifted children tend to be very introspective. They like to take time to process events and mull them over. Allow your child the space that she needs to think things through. If there is something that it is important to you to talk about, set a time and date in advance. This shows respect for your child's need for space, while not allowing her to control the situation.

Children will always require correction, as the nature of parenting requires. Children need leadership and authority to provide them with security. Too much freedom and decision making before it is developmentally appropriate leads to many problems in the future. Parents should control much of the decision making and responsibilities when children are younger, and children should gain decision-making power as well as responsibilities as they mature and grow older. When children make mistakes, parents need to correct them as a part of teaching them. When providing correction, try to remember the sandwich principle. Start with a compliment, follow with a gentle rebuke, and then back with another praise. For example, "I really like how hard you are working at being organized with your schoolwork. It seems to me, though, that you forgot to turn in your permission slip for the field trip on time. As a consequence of forgetting, you will have to miss the field trip. Maybe you could write yourself a reminder in your planner—you have been doing a great job keeping track of school assignments that way. How else can I help you stay organized?" Hold your child accountable, praise their successes, and continue to offer to help in any way you can. While this is much easier to say than to enforce, the most powerful teaching tools in a parent's repertoire are logical consequences. These logical consequences to problem behaviors provide powerful lasting memories that will help your child grow in her understanding of responsibility and consequences.

No one likes to be constantly harassed for her performance. If you had to have a daily review with your boss instead of an annual one, you might start to get a little frustrated. Your child feels the same way. The purpose of talking with your child is to build a relationship. While you won't treat her the same way you would a friend, you should still treat her as a person. Constantly nagging your child about her grades, her friends, and her life does not build a relationship. Try to build an open-communication relationship where both parties have freedom to talk as well as listen to the other party. This is not suggesting in any way that children should treat or view their parents as peers or friends, but that parents and children should strive to be able to communicate freely. Parents must remain authority figures in order for family balance and discipline to be effective. However, parents can communicate with friendliness and respect while maintaining their position of authority.

Finally, enough cannot be said about praising your child. Think about your conversations. Which bosses do you like and respect the most: those who complain and criticize all the time or those who are creative and interesting with their input? Find ways to honestly praise your child for her efforts while constructively providing feedback when needed.

⊜ Alert

While praise is important, make sure to avoid artificial accolades. Gifted children can see right through insincerity. The key to giving effective praise is to really know your child—her strengths and her weaknesses. Recognizing her strengths is okay, but can lead to hollow praise. A child who has been riding a bike for several years does not need to be told she is doing well. Knowing what areas your child has difficulty with and praising her for her true efforts will go far in building a healthy relationship.

Communicating with Other Adults

Your child will encounter many adults in his life outside of his parents. Teachers, uncles, coaches, and others will fill his life. Adults should be treated with a certain level of respect, which can be difficult for gifted children to master. Try to make this as concrete as possible for your child from a young age. Start with a list of three things your child should always do when he is speaking with adult. Perhaps you choose: shake their hand as a greeting, look them in the eyes when speaking, and answer their questions with a complete sentence. Even young preschoolers can begin to master these three steps when they are practiced, expected, and enforced. Later on, you can add other steps for older children as these are mastered. You might add responding to requests with, "Yes, sir" or "Yes, ma'am" or making sure to greet all adults as they enter the home or classroom. Each family can decide which particular signs of cordiality are important for interactions with adults.

Helping your child learn to speak clearly and respectfully to adults will improve the way he communicates with others as well as the way others perceive him. You can explain it to your child exactly that way. Gifted children respond well to clear instructions with meaningful explanations. They certainly dislike, "Because I said so" as a response, even more vehemently than other children. Most gifted children prefer the company of adults, but adults often interact condescendingly or dismissively to children. By teaching your child some basic practices for communicating with adults, you will help him to build better relationships with those adults he comes into contact with. You can also teach your child what topics are appropriate to converse about as well as what topics are typically considered socially unacceptable. Many gifted children are inherently drawn to more adult conversation topics; however, it is important to speak with your child about refraining from initiating conversations on politics, religion, finances, and other taboo subjects. Helping your child know that these are not usually spoken about in general company will keep them from experiencing awkward encounters with both adults and peers. Additionally, make sure you teach your child how to disagree with someone without making the entire conversation uncomfortable and disagreeable.

Alert

As with any parenting practice, the key to success is clear expectations coupled with consistent consequences. Gifted children may have difficulty looking someone in the eyes or speaking clearly. Continue to practice these skills, expect them every time, and have a set consequence for when expectations are not met. Some possible consequences might include sitting out for a short time at an activity to think about appropriate behaviors or perhaps writing a list of reminders to be reviewed before the next family outing.

Communicating with Peers

Gifted children tend to prefer the company of adults, because adults are easier for many gifted kids to interact with. Age-level peers tend not to understand gifted children, with their extensive vocabularies, seemingly strange interests, and single-minded focus on a subject. Adults tend to overlook the quirks of gifted children in ways their peers do not. While a few caring and supportive adults in a child's life can make a huge difference, your child should also have at least a few peers as friends.

Most in the gifted community encourage parents to help their children build relationships with other kids by finding like-minded children with whom they can forge friendships. While this is important in helping your child build lasting and meaningful relationships, it does not necessarily help your gifted child learn to live within the predominant culture. Parents can help their children develop the skills they need to be friends with children who are not gifted, as well. Talking with your child about the qualities that friends have and how she can demonstrate those in play situations can help her. When parents explain to their gifted child how certain behaviors are perceived by others, it can help gifted children establish a set of rules and a hierarchy for their own behavior that can help them navigate the tricky waters of mainstream friendships.

It may also be helpful to set up play dates with families that you are friends with whose children are not gifted. If the parents have already established a rapport, it may be easier to assist both children in how to be friends without the awkwardness of trying to communicate with a random parent from school who is unfamiliar with your child or your circumstances.

Showing Your Child How to Make Friends

There are many things you can do as a parent to help your child learn the invaluable skill of making friends. Young gifted children benefit from being exposed to other young gifted children regardless of gender. Don't worry if your daughter is drawn to boys or your son to girls. Gifted children flock to intelligence wherever they can find it, regardless of age or gender. Gifted children seem to be more supportive of the special characteristics of other gifted children such as their intensity and sensory issues. You can help your child build relationships with peers who are not gifted, as well. Teaching basic social skills helps tremendously. Many young gifted children do not pick up on social cues from others. Help your child learn about personal space, voice regulation, and smiling. In addition, practice having a back-and-forth dialogue as opposed to your child dominating the conservation with her own interests. One visual example you can share with your child is that of throwing a ball back and forth. Grab a tennis ball or basketball, and explain that each time she says something, she should pass the ball to someone else and let them have a turn to talk.

During the adolescent years, most of your child's peers will separate into same-gender friendship groups. This can cause problems for gifted students who simply draw on a smaller pool of resources. At this time, helping your child become involved in a group or club with students who share similar interests can be critical. It may take a few tries to find a group where she clicks, but exposing her to different interests in hopes of finding a safe space within the early teenage years is important. There are many different groups to try: Math Counts, Odyssey of the Mind, sports, martial arts, drama, school newspaper, Boy Scouts, Girl Scouts, or school yearbooks are a few examples. Parents can even consider starting their own special-interest group—local libraries are always eager and willing to host these groups.

 **Essential**

Gifted children are particularly influenced by seeing and hearing about models and examples. You can find great books about friendship that reinforce both good and bad examples. Reading books and talking about how friendship looks with your child will help teach the social skills your child needs to be successful—without you having to think up the examples or scenarios to provide discussion! Don't overdo it, but maybe one or two books and conversations a week, especially after a summer break or before a play date, should do the trick.

Leta Hollingworth, a pioneer in the field of gifted education, noted that the strongest feelings of isolation for gifted children occurred between the ages of four and nine. While this may be a universal longing, it's harder for gifted children, since they are outliers in many ways. Parents need to be aware of the intensity of the feelings of being alone that their child may be experiencing during these years. Because of their advanced intellectual age coupled with the intensity of their feelings, gifted children are acutely aware of being isolated. Current studies have shown that having even one "true friend" can make a powerful difference in a child's sense of belonging. This is especially true for children in a mainstream school setting where some of the power of a family unit can be diminished by limited time together. In families that are especially close knit or that homeschool, familial and sibling bonds can take the place of a close friend children in a school setting need.

Learning with Your Child
How to Handle Conflict

Parents should also be careful about stepping in to handle their child's conflicts. While this is helpful in some situations, gifted children need to learn to handle difficulties and troubles on their own. Often they can become steadfast and inflexible if they are convinced they are right. A parent stepping in can reinforce this and keep their child from learning how to negotiate, compromise, and problem solve. Many times, adults and other children see gifted children as know-it-alls. Allowing your child to handle minor conflicts on her own can teach her valuable communication skills.

Teaching Your Child
How to Handle Relatives

One of the most trying relationships for gifted families can be surprising to hear. Many parents of gifted children express that their families are the most difficult to deal with regarding their child's giftedness.

Grandparents in particular can feel defensive of parents' choices for their child. The defensiveness most often comes from a place of self-judgment. When a parent makes a certain choice that may be different from the choice his own parents made, grandparents can feel that this is an indictment against their own parenting. Gifted children can feel caught in the middle between parents and grandparents. Parents can help alleviate this by validating their parents' choices while explaining the reasoning behind their own alternate choices. For example, saying, "Mom, I know you sent me to public school, and I learned a lot there. But for Joey, we think homeschooling is the best choice, for his particular needs and gifts." Make sure that your statement is well thought out, to avoid overemotional discourses. Also, you can support your statement with positive outcomes that may come from your decision, including how it will affect the grandparents' roles as well.

 Alert

Times have changed since most of your parents were in school. Grandparents sometimes assume things are the same now as they once were for children, which is not the case. Sometimes simply explaining all the new opportunities your child has available as well as the new research on how the gifted brain learns and thrives can be enough to help ease familial tensions.

Animosities can extend to aunts, uncles, and other relatives, as well. Parenting can become a case of too many cooks in the kitchen, with everyone wanting to offer his input on exactly what is the best way to guide a child. Others may also feel a sense of competition between their own children and yours. This can make family gatherings intense! Helping your child have a healthy self-confidence and assurance in which they are will provide insulation in these instances. Do not feel the need to train your child to hide who he is in order to fit in, but at the same time remain cognizant of these issues if they exist in your family. You can talk with your child prior to family gatherings about activities and interests the whole family shares. Review good communication strategies so that he does not monopolize conversation with his interests and further alienate himself. While it may not eradicate the problems you may be experiencing, it can help keep it from taking center stage at family get-togethers.

As with any parenting issue, remaining positive but firm is key. You are the parent, and you bear the ultimate responsibility for your child. Try to explain your decisions where you feel necessary, but remain resolute. You can also make sure to communicate your parenting choices in such a way that leaves no room for the interference of relatives. When unsolicited advice is offered, quickly and firmly change the subject.

This will help minimize your child's tug-of-war experience. Parents may also need to talk to grandparents and relatives about not going to the child behind their back or undermining their parental authority. In situations where this occurs, help your child learn to redirect relatives back to you. Your child may develop a habit of saying something like, "Oh, Grandpa, you know that Mom likes you to talk to her because I am not in charge of making decisions." This gently lets the grandparent know that the child is not in control and also that the relative knows they should be speaking to the parent instead of the child. If you feel your child can handle it, teach him how to explain what decisions you as a family have made.

Essential

Some families struggle with this less than others. Many are able to incorporate the helpful advice of caring extended family members. For parents who like to discuss difficult choices with relatives, they can let those concerned relatives know that while their input is appreciated, the final decision is left up to the parents who have ultimate authority over the child.

Often, giving grandparents and relatives a way to participate can help them feel involved. Perhaps a grandparent can teach his grandchild woodworking, bird watching, or another interest that he has that the child finds intriguing. As a parent, keep in mind that the interests of older folks and children do not always mesh. The child might need to be exposed to it more than once before finding such an activity intriguing or interesting. The optimal situation would be for the grandparent to share her passion in such a way that it is contagious to the grandchild. But if there isn't one or a particular interest does not click, then they could find something to learn together or the grandparent could pass along some life skills—cooking, sewing, investing, anything that would give them a commonality. Families can also work together on shared family histories through genealogies and the recording of family stories, which allows youngsters to demonstrate proficiency with technology while giving their elders a chance to share the past with the next generation. Encourage local grandparents to help attend children's activities and school performances. Have your child write handwritten invitations and send thank-you notes after, when appropriate.

Relatives who do not live in the same geographical area can still be positively involved. Tape events for them to watch. Set up regular online video conferences. Help your child create digital story books and recordings for them. If the grandparent in your life is not technologically skilled, try sending letters through regular mail or making routine phone calls. When you visit, consider taking along the supplies to be able to share videos and pictures with her.

Making sure your children have a healthy and positive relationship with their grandparents is important for establishing intergenerational ties and developing their sense of familial history. This also helps your child feel a sense of belonging to your family and to the larger world. By exerting just a little extra effort and helping your child as well, you can foster a lifelong connection between your child and your parents.

Your Child and Teachers

One of the most important relationships any child can have is with her teacher. Children spend as much if not more of their waking hours with teachers as they do with their families. That is why this relationship is so significant, and also a factor in why many families decide to homeschool. Additionally, for most children, forming a relationship with a teacher is a process that will take place annually. In middle school and high school, the ability to build a relationship with a teacher becomes even more important, as children juggle multiple teachers, some changing each semester. Helping your children learn to build positive, working relationships with their teachers is a skill that will enrich all their school years and carry over into future real-world situations.

There are some difficulties that can take place between a gifted child and her teacher. Teachers often see gifted children as lazy, unmotivated, messy, off task, and a host of other related characteristics that can cause teachers to dislike gifted students. These are most likely related to a child's giftedness; however, you can see how a teacher would consider such a child a problem in the classroom, since they have many other students to work with simultaneously. This can lead to friction establishing a healthy relationship with the teacher.

🔔 Alert

It is very common for gifted children to feel as though people need to earn their respect. This can pose problems for adults who do not understand gifted children. Additionally, gifted children may also think that those who are not as intelligent as they are do not warrant respect. Teach your child about general respect that we offer to everyone—common courtesies, polite manners, etc. Help them to understand that there are certain niceties extended to everyone as part of a civilized nature. You may approach this through a discussion with your child on how different people have different strengths. Some are highly intelligent while others are physically gifted. Some are particularly sensitive and kind while other are determined and strong in perseverance. You can instill in your child that every person is deserving of respect.

As the parent of a gifted child, you can help him overcome these struggles in many ways. First, carry over the manners for communicating with adults discussed previously in this chapter. Teachers are adults, and should be given the same respect that other adults are given. Parents should instill in their children an understanding that teachers are deserving of more respect than run-of-the-mill adults, since they've been placed in a position of authority over the child, temporarily ceded to them while the children are in their care instead of the parents'.

Teachers are not the only people with unreasonable expectations that your child will ever face. Later in life, employers, spouses, and friends can also offer relational challenges. It is important for your child to learn to cope within society if she hopes to be successful someday. Teaching your child certain interpersonal skills such as patience, sensitivity, and perseverance in relationships from a young age can be very beneficial. Giftedness offers us an explanation as to why this might be more difficult for some children. However, it is important for your child to learn that her giftedness is not an excuse; it's a reason to work harder, knowing that the ability is there.

Some small factors may help your child be successful in relating to a teacher. From the preschool age, teach your child to be orderly. Having a schedule for the day, along with pictures to correspond, helps your young child to order his day and prepares him for the schedules of school.

❗ Alert

It is also good to occasionally make variations to your schedule to teach your child flexibility, since deviations from expected sequence can cause problems for gifted children who are accustomed to order. These interruptions can also happen in a regular school day, so your child will need to be prepared for them. Try to plan a family outing, play date, or something else unique a few times a month to offer your child a chance to learn coping mechanisms for change.

Helping your child learn to organize her toys and belongings at home can also help her be organized at school. Children as young as nine months can begin to help around the house by picking up toys and placing them into bins labeled with pictures, turning off lights, and taking out small trashcans at her level throughout the house—the responsibilities can grow as your child does. Being responsible is important in being a student, in building relationships, and in later adult life. Teachers appreciate students who are independent and respectful of their things and those of others, as do family members, friends, and future spouses.

There is a big difference between conforming to society and behaving appropriately in a given setting. Some people may feel that teaching your child to be responsible may stifle their creativity, squash their personality, or diminish their individuality. In the words of Eleanor Roosevelt, "Nobody can make you feel inferior without your consent." Giving your child responsibilities will not make her feel inferior unless it is done in such a way as to minimize who she is or her special talents. Parents can teach their children that their strengths are in their own perceptions of who they are, not in what others think. Life is filled with rules and regulations, most of which are not of our making. Helping your child learn to navigate these constraints while remaining true to herself is an essential step toward parenting a child who can manage in society. Parents can also keep in mind that there are usually multiple ways to achieve a goal, and different people will choose various methods, so the student needs to learn to clarify with the teacher whether it's important to follow the teacher's process or if the student is allowed to decide on her own way to accomplish the task. It's imperative to make clear to your child the idea of integrity and that she must talk with you if anything the teacher says conflicts with the values the family holds. If you are uncomfortable with the rules of a particular teacher and feel personally conflicted about having your child follow them, move your child to another teacher's classroom or another school. Otherwise, it is important that you teach your child how to follow that teacher's rules, demonstrate proper behavior, and follow these both up with supportive parenting at home.

Parents need to set a positive example at home, as well. Speak positively about the teacher and see disagreements in the best possible light, which will model good communication for your child. Your child will always take your lead. If you don't like your child's teacher or speak ill of him in front of your child, it will set the standard for your child. Children often repeat what's said at home later on to the teacher, which can create a cycle of negative feelings.

Remember, the better the relationship your child has with her teacher the more likely she is to be successful in school. As a parent, taking these steps to nurture that positive relationship can help ensure your child maintains a positive relationship with their educators.

CHAPTER 15

Intensity and the Gifted Child

G ifted children are not the same as regular children. This is
true in many ways, but one of the most prominent ways this
manifests itself is in the intensity of a gifted child. They concentrate
harder and they get more easily distracted. They laugh harder and
cry longer. They fight longer and more passionately. Sometimes it
seems as though every ounce of their being is tightly wound and
directed completely at whatever they are doing.

Dabrowski's Theories on Intensity

Kazimierz Dabrowski was a Polish psychologist around the time of
the first and second world wars. He coined the term Over Excitabil-
ities (sometimes abbreviated as OEs) with regard to gifted children.
This term is commonly used in contemporary gifted communities
to refer to the intensities that a gifted child often experiences.

How It Manifests

Overexcitabilities have to do with how the brain reacts to a
stimulus. There are normal reactions, and then there are overre-
actions. According to Dabrowski, in a gifted child or adult's brain,
there is an overreaction to a seemingly normal stimulus. These
are what he termed overexcitabilities. You may have experienced
this in a variety of ways with your gifted child. They refuse to wear

socks because the seam bothers them. Many gifted children dislike jeans because the texture is too harsh. Your child complains about the noise on the school bus hurting his ears. These are just a few examples of how a gifted brain can be overprocessing a sensation that does not bother another child.

ⓔ❗ Alert

If you would like to learn more about the work of Kazimierz Dabrowski, his research has been adapted into the book *Living with Intensity: Understanding the Sensitivity, Excitability, and the Emotional Development of Gifted Children, Adolescents, and Adults*, edited by Susan Daniels and Michael M. Piechowski.

Psychologists highlight three primary ways for gifted children to categorize their experiences: they can feel a greater level of intensity to something, have a stronger sensitivity to a stimulus, or may become overexcited by a given stimulus.

Intensity

Intensity refers to the strength of the response to a stimulus. This can be expressed a variety of ways. A gifted child may have an emotional response—becoming very happy, very sad, or very frustrated by an experience or encounter. Gifted children can have a physical or somatic response by getting a headache or stomach-ache as a result of a particular stress in their lives. They can also develop fears or anxieties about something they have learned or discovered. These may seem irrational to others, but make perfect sense to a gifted child. In extreme situations, professional counseling may be needed in order to help a gifted child work through such trials. Finally, intensity can manifest itself in strong memories about previous occurrences. Your child might make mountains out of molehills, but you should also recognize that one child's molehill might honestly be another child's mountain. Gifted children experience intensities in a variety of ways beyond these examples.

Sensitivity

Gifted children are especially sensitive, as well. They are very in tune to the troubles of the world and social injustice. Gifted children worry about homeless people and the poor, wondering why no one does anything. They take on the pain of the afflicted for themselves, demonstrating high levels of empathy. Some children become fixated on one particular social issue while others take on all the problems of the world and are sensitive to many different plights of underprivileged and oppressed people.

Overexcitability

Dabrowski highlighted five primary areas where gifted children can experience overstimulation to a relatively normal stimulus, which he termed overexcitability.

The first area is psychomotor. This refers to the need for more physical activity. It seems as though your child bounces off the wall. He cannot sit still while he is working. While talking to you, he bounces on one foot and waves his hands excessively. He is characterized by nervous gestures and odd mannerisms. Parents can help children with this issue by having them sit on an exercise ball while working or by making sure to take time for gross-motor skills activities regularly.

The second area of overexcitability is sensual. Anything that deals with the five senses in a strong way would be sensual overexcitability. Sensual overexcitabilities relate to any stimulus from the five senses. These are the children who love the invention of tagless T-shirts, and their mothers are thankful not to have to clip the tags off any longer. Your daughter may insist on wearing only skirts because pants strangle her. She cannot share a bedroom with her sister because the sound of another person breathing is like the roaring of an ocean to her. The smell of the roast cooking in the slow cooker may overwhelm her from across the house. Children who experience sensual overexcitabilities are also especially aware of color, texture, and tiny harmonies in music. They have a deep and profound appreciation for the natural beauty of life. Your daughter may cry easily at music, be deeply moved by a piece of art, laugh uncontrollably at a story, or need a special cuddling blanket well past childhood. To address these concerns, parents can let their child know that they are not alone in this world and that they need to develop their own focusing skills. That may be having a sound machine or fan blowing at night, using earplugs to drown out noise, or practicing deep-breathing activities. Parents and children can work together to find strategies that provide relief for the individual as well as for the good of the family.

Gifted children may also experience imaginational overexcitability. Children who are imaginationally overexcitable often seem lost in the clouds. They love anything fantastical and can become lost in books for hours. Their brain has an inordinate ability to visualize the unseen. These children grow up to be writers and inventors, seeing the world as it could be instead of as it is.

Essential

Family game nights can provide a wonderful time for those with intellectual excitability. They are also a time to practice fair play, winning graciously, and losing graciously. This is a chance for parents to allow children to see each other's varying strengths and weaknesses.

Another area for overexcitability is intellectual. Most gifted children experience this type of overexcitability. They love puzzles and word play, brain teasers and riddles. They have an insatiable thirst for knowledge, and learning excites them in a way that is almost visceral. Your son may come home literally bursting to share what he discovered in science class, read in his textbook, or heard through a guest speaker. Parents can hone these skills by providing ample opportunities to practice them through the use of Highlights Math Mania and geography magazines, puzzle books, and problem-solving activities.

The final area where overexcitability may occur is emotional. Gifted children feel emotions in a deeper and more fundamental way. When they are sad, they are extremely sad—crying easily at books, movies, or stories on the news. When they are happy, they radiate happiness like the sun. This can manifest itself in a need for close relationships as an outlet for sharing these deep emotions. Gifted children can even invent imaginary playmates or imaginary relationships to create an avenue for these feelings. These extreme highs and lows can also make gifted children more susceptible to depression and peer pressure, so parents should remain alert to prolonged changes in behavior.

Why Are Gifted Kids so Intense?

Dabrowski and other psychologists have done a tremendous amount of research on the intensity of gifted children. You may be asking yourself, "Well, *why* is my child so intense?" The answer is simple: They just are. Their brain is hardwired to be that way. They can no more change this aspect of their identity than they can change their eye color or height.

Parents need to remember that this is not something their child is doing to cause problems or annoy them. These feelings are very real for your child. She is not making them up, but is truly feeling these strong sensations and emotions. She is as overwhelmed by feeling them as you are to responding to them. Imagine experiencing the whole world in high definition with all of your senses. It might seem like an exciting way to live for a few short hours in a movie, but if you had to do it all the time, you might quickly grow tired of it. That is a lot to process all the time. This is your child's everyday experience. It takes an enormous amount of energy just to live life immersed in such strong feelings all the time.

Try to respond to your child with compassion and sensitivity. Your child is most likely doing the very best that she can to handle these overexcitabilities. While understanding them does not excuse her responses, you can work with your child to learn how to process these feelings and emotions in healthy and beneficial ways. Seeing the world so intensely is a wonderful gift, and you can help your child use it responsibly. Parents should also know that gifted children learn early that this high level of sensitivity is different. They may begin to think there is something wrong with them for feeling this way when others don't. Many also become inaccurately diagnosed with depression. You can let your gifted child know that intensity is a common experience for other gifted children. Allow her to talk through her feelings and experiences to validate them as real.

How to Harness Intensity for Good

Parents can find it terribly difficult to understand and help a child who cares so passionately about most topics. There are some ways you can assist your child in learning to handling these strong feelings. First off, you can help him develop an emotions-based vocabulary. Knowing clear words to describe these emotions can help relieve the pressure of those feelings. Teach him words like "rage," "frustration," and "impatience" as well others that can truly capture the feelings he might be experiencing.

Journaling is also a powerful tool for managing the intense experiences of being gifted. Some children benefit from journaling daily while others need this outlet on a more sporadic basis. Another possible tool for your child is a dialogue journal, where he writes you a letter and you respond. Leaving the updated dialogue journal under each other's pillow to read and respond to is a good way to encourage reflection. Talking through how a person is feeling is a cathartic exchange. There are also some specific activities that can help a gifted child positively express these intense feelings.

 **Essential**

Young children can also benefit from learning to express their feelings. Some younger children like to attach a color to their feelings. They can express feeling blue for sadness, yellow for happiness, green for excited, etc. This is another way for a creative child to be able to process the intense emotions she might be having. Your young child may also enjoy the picture book *Feelings* by Aliki for another concrete way to share what she might be experiencing.

Volunteerism

Many children find a satisfying outlet for their intensity in doing volunteer work. This allows them to feel as though they are making a difference righting the injustices of the world that are plaguing them. The problems that they see all around them are no longer insurmountable and emotionally overwhelming. They are a challenge and an opportunity for him to make the world better.

 Alert

As a parent, try to find a community organization that matches the causes your child feels strongly about. If your child is concerned about the poor and homeless, volunteer at a soup kitchen as a family or organize a clothing drive. If your child worries about the environment, find a group that plants trees or cleans up litter. While volunteering in general is good, tying your service to the area that your child cares about is what makes this a meaningful experience and helps her process her strong feelings.

Community Leadership Opportunities

Another way that many gifted children find to harness their intensity is through community leadership opportunities. This can start at a young age, with student council or a school newspaper. Gifted children are often natural leaders because of their passion and devotion. Your child can use those skills to become a leader in her school and community. If your school does not have some of these opportunities, try to help your child create them on her own. There are also community organizations like Boy Scouts and Girl Scouts with further chances for leadership and community involvement. She can write a newspaper for your neighborhood or pass out flyers about a cause.

 **Essential**

The process of running for office or applying for a position in a club can be an excellent learning opportunity in taking appropriate risks. This is an important life lesson, and while your child may fail to secure a position, she will have laid the groundwork for confronting life challenges that may come her way.

Creative Arts

Exploring the creative arts is another path you can encourage your child along to help her manage her strong feelings. Many children benefit from being enrolled in art classes. Your local parks and recreations department might offer classes on a quarterly or other basis. These are great for exposing your child to a wide range of mediums: oil painting, watercolors, and ceramics. A school art teacher or guidance counselor may also be able to direct you to local fine arts programs. Additionally, your child may enjoy attending poetry or creative writing course or group. Artistic activities can allow a child a form of self-expression without having to discuss her feelings in person or while trying to use words. Processing information this way is particularly helpful for children who are shy or have difficulty sharing how they are reacting. Some groups even offer parent-child versions that might be a fun endeavor for you and your child to participate in together.

 Alert

Parents should be aware that gifted children often want to give up quickly in these activities if they feel they are not good enough or becoming good enough, fast enough to suit them. Let your child know that he is obligated to complete the course if he begins it. Remind him that most people are not good at everything immediately. Activities can be enjoyable just because you are doing them and finding pleasure in the activity, not because you are the very best at whatever you may be attempting.

In the middle and high school years, creative activities are often available through your local school system. In the younger years, and for children who desire a more intense version, you can look outside the school system to local artisans or community groups to provide this instruction.

Why Intensity Starts Not to Matter

Fortunately for your child, there is hope! These intensity characteristics of passion, resoluteness, and sensitivity that cause problems for children are what make successful adults. As children grow and learn, they begin to develop skills for processing these strong emotions. These passions become what drive adults to do exciting things in their careers and free time. Gifted children grow up to discover cures for diseases, advocate for governmental change, and invent new products for the marketplace. They become politicians, humanitarians, and distinguished businessmen and businesswomen. Where once their classmates were put off by their strong feelings, now the world takes notice.

🛑 Alert

The book *Cradles of Eminence: Childhoods of More than 700 Famous Men and Women* by Victor Goertzel is an excellent read for families who would like to learn more about prestigious examples like Eleanor Roosevelt, Albert Einstein, and Thomas Edison, who overcame many obstacles in their youths to become great figures in history.

It is important for your child to know that childhood is temporary. Eventually, a day will come when their gifts and talents will be celebrated by the world. Many children find this type of long-term payoff hard to fathom, but other children find it helpful to know that there is a time coming in the future when life will not be so hard.

It is important that you help your child learn how to process his intense emotions. When a child does not learn healthy expressions for his emotions, he may begin to build unhealthy patterns. These are evidenced in frequent emotional outbursts, withdrawing from loved ones, or inappropriate responses in social settings. If you help your child learn these coping mechanisms for the strong emotions he is feeling, he will grow up to be a socially well adjusted and caring person.

CHAPTER 16

Perfectionism and the Gifted Child

One of the prominent traits of a gifted child is perfectionism. It seems that being a perfectionist and being gifted often go hand in hand. Many see perfectionism as a positive trait, while others are concerned about the potential life-long ramifications of perfectionism. Regardless of your viewpoint, as a parent of a gifted child you need to be equipped with information on perfectionism.

What Is Perfectionism?

Perfectionists want to be perfect. Some people can be perfectionists in a single subject or in a single area while others are perfectionists by their very nature. Perfectionists have strong ideals and can visualize the goal that they have for themselves for a given task. They are determined to make that vision a reality. Often, perfectionists do not just want to do a task perfectly, they desire to do it better than anyone else has ever done it.

Gifted children are particularly prone to become perfectionists for a variety of reasons. Primarily, gifted children have a strong sense of purpose and vision. When given a problem or task they can quickly determine several possible solutions then mentally visualize and sort them to find the best one. Having done so, they set about making the solution they visualize a reality. This is where perfectionism comes in: gifted children are unable to settle for anything less than their mental ideal, leading to a need to be perfect. They may also demand perfection from those around them. Perfectionists also refuse to believe that a work is finished; forced to complete it by a deadline, they are rarely satisfied with the end result.

Additionally, gifted children are usually strongly motivated to succeed. From a young age, they become used to processing and applying new information quickly and with ease. When they are younger, this becomes their habit. As they get older, they continue to expect themselves to be able to rise to the top in every endeavor they face. Even as challenges become more difficult, the desire to remain above their peers pushes them to attempt perfection. What sets perfectionism apart from a healthy drive to succeed is the irrational desire to attain perfection at whatever the cost, and the inability to move beyond life's natural failures. In case you are still on the fence with regard to whether or not perfectionism is a healthy habit, consider the dangerous side effects. It can lead to health issues such as stomach troubles, headaches, and insomnia. Additionally, perfectionists may be afraid to try new things for fear they will fail. Parents can teach their children the mantra, "Better to do something badly than not to do something at all."

What Causes Perfectionism?

There are several factors that can cause perfectionism. Children who have grown up in a family that frequently praises even trivial accomplishments can become perfectionists. They may feel that they are only valued for their performance and not for who they are as a person. Additionally, children who have siblings or parents who are successful can become perfectionists in an attempt to live up to a perceived family standard of performance. This is often the case with gifted children who have highly accomplished families. Being admitted to a strenuous academic program can lead to perfectionism, as students are faced with competition to be the best as well as the feeling that they have to perform well to validate their acceptance to the program, and examples of other students who may be equally or more talented than they are.

Another factor influencing perfectionism in gifted children is the role of the parent. Parents of gifted children are often stereotyped as pushy, demanding, and intense. These stereotypes can be rightfully earned for some parents. Some parents expect a level of performance akin to perfection, in every area.

Additionally, a child who has survived some type of extraordinary event or trauma may also suffer from perfectionism. This results from a desire to control his environment in order to protect himself from future pain.

A child who has been taught to value the opinions of others will be more prone to perfection as he struggles to receive affirmation and validation for his performance. Perfectionism can become a vicious cycle of setting unrealistic goals and expectations, feeling as though you failed to meet them, and creating even more unattainable goals based on those failures.

Why Is Perfectionism a Problem?

Most people have a certain idea of what perfectionism is—a very smart, detail-oriented individual motivated to succeed. On the surface, it doesn't sound bad and may even sound like qualities you should strive toward. However, beneath the surface, perfectionism can cause serious problems.

Perfectionism becomes a problem when it becomes all consuming. The goal ceases to be learning and starts to become perfection. Children are no longer intrinsically motivated by the joy of acquiring new skills and information, but are solely motivated by their grade or their performance on tasks. This is a superficial type of motivation that eventually reaches a crux.

Perfectionism at its heart is a prideful condition. A child can become so focused on her own performance that she fails to recognize her place within her family and society. All relationships become contests where the perfectionist is either better or worse than those around her, living in a constant state of judgment that is hardly conducive to healthy relationships. This type of stress can lead to physiological symptoms, as well.

Another problem with perfectionism is that it changes a child's identity. Children who are perfectionists define their sense of self by being perfect. Any time they fail to meet their standard of perfection, it challenges who they are as individuals. They fear failure, avoid taking natural risks, and begin to shut down in order to protect themselves from losing their identity. These protective mechanisms are somewhat complicated, and it requires individual attention to fully understand their consequences to a gifted child.

Limiting Possibilities

Perfectionism becomes a problem when it limits a child's possibilities. Perfectionists tend to become specialists in one or two strength areas. They stick to these areas and try to become better and better at them. This keeps them from exploring new possibilities. It also inhibits their ability to grow and develop as a dynamic individual. They may have one bad experience in writing, which convinces them that they could never be a writer. This keeps them from ever pushing through that one experience to find the joy in writing that may be there. Unfortunately, society gives mixed messages by valuing the specialist, but not the generalist. The emphasis as a parent should be on your child not closing herself off to other possibilities at too young an age and on learning to accept lesser standards of performance in nonspecialty areas.

Fearing Failure

The fear of failure becomes a source of great anxiety for perfectionists. They are so tied to the idea of being perfect that they refuse to try any new subject they may not be perfect at immediately. Another way this may manifest itself is in the child trying new things, but quickly quitting them if she does not feel she is acquiring the new skill fast enough. Countless young people, especially young women, avoid careers in math and science because such fields are difficult and require effort. Perfectionists are afraid to try and fail, so they simply do not try anything that does not come easily to them.

❓ Question

How can parents keep their children from allowing the fear of failure to limit their opportunities?
Parents can take some simple steps to help their children in this area from a young age. Make sure your child is exposed to a variety of extracurricular areas. If your child is good at sports, have them take an art class. Make sure that your child knows at the start of the activity that he must follow through to the point of completion, no matter what. This builds strength of character and helps him see the value in participating in activities for the sake of enjoyment instead of superior performance.

Meltdowns

An emotional consequence of perfectionism can be meltdowns. This is particularly true in the early years for a gifted child. The strong ability to envision an end-product becomes an albatross around the neck for a perfectionist. Gifted children know what quality work looks like, but may find they are unable to produce such work because of the limitations of their knowledge or physical development. When a teacher or parent requests a certain outcome, a gifted child may think they are expected to produce that higher level of product, and become emotionally upset at the prospect of being unable to attain it. Some children process these emotions through crying, others through angry outburst, and still others withdraw. Many underachieving gifted students are actually perfectionists at heart who are refusing to try for fear that they will fail. Withdrawal is the only way they know to cope with the emotions that they are feeling, having never learned healthier outlets for expressing themselves. Parents can teach their children to understand that learning is a process and not just an assignment that is finished once and then done.

Dangerous Consequences

Perfectionism can start out as a relatively innocent desire to do your best. Sadly, it does not typically stop there. Perfectionism can escalate into scary behaviors. Perfectionists can begin to become angry and unable to accept their mistakes and the mistakes of others. They react disproportionately to the circumstances that can drive a wedge into relationships as friends and family members feel the perfectionist pushing their unrealistic standards onto others. Perfectionists can also become highly driven. They put excessive demands on themselves and pursue them to exclusion of all else in their lives. A perfectionist can never be satisfied with what they have done, always seeing the problems and errors or how it could have been better instead of appreciating their products and efforts, such as the tendency to habitually focus on one spot on the newly painted wall rather than on the overall result of a beautifully painted room.

Perfectionism can also lead to more serious issues. Perfectionists can be at a greater risk for eating disorders, as they strive to be physically perfect no matter the cost. They can be more susceptible to difficulties with alcohol and drugs as well as other destructive behaviors, as they attempt to find an escape from the world they have created for themselves. A perfectionist may also suffer from depression as he fights the idea of never being good enough. Perfectionists can also sabotage their school and work efforts with their demands that others meet their same performance and drive. Perfectionist tendencies can result in an individual developing a poor self-image, seeing only his failures and never his successes, which can lead to a terribly unsatisfied life.

Fact

Interestingly enough, recent studies have shown that students who are identified as perfectionists do not actually perform better than students who are not perfectionists. So, even if perfectionism is considered a positive trait in some circles, it is not producing any better results than students who do not approach their work this way.

Problems Perfectionists Face

Perfectionists can face many different problems in their lives. Not surprisingly, a perfectionist is often lonely. She spends so much time pursuing perfection that she has little time left over for people and relationships. Additionally, she often drives away the people in her life through her angry and demanding behaviors.

Perfectionists are also driven to be flawless. This is an unhealthy mentality because making mistakes is an important part of learning and growing. A perfectionist limits herself from becoming a truly great person through her refusal to accept natural and normal mistakes and limitations.

Another problem that a perfectionist can face is the tendency to be judgmental. She desires for everything in her environment to be perfect, and is constantly on the lookout for the failings and inabilities of others around her. She can be rigid and uncompromising in her beliefs and refuse to allow others to make mistakes, as well. This can lead to strained relationships and a lack of compassion for others. Perfectionists are also tired. It takes a lot of work to maintain their perfect image, and they are always on guard for any possible slip up. This can eventually become exhausting.

How to Recognize Perfectionism

Parents can watch for warning signs in order to address and correct perfectionism early on, before their child faces some of these terrible consequences. A gifted perfectionist may request correction fluid to ensure no one can see he wrote something different initially. He may request to redo a task if he did not receive a perfect or high enough score. Your child may hide a test paper that does not have a perfect score on it. A young perfectionist may attempt a task, and tear up multiple attempts if a small mistake was made. Your child wants to rehash or discuss mistakes over and over, and seems unable to let go. Perfectionists are afraid to ask for help completing a task, fearing that this shows weakness. A perfectionist commonly points out your mistakes and those of people around you, but becomes angry or withdraws when he is corrected. These are just a few of the initial warning signs parents can look for to determine if their child might be a perfectionist.

How Perfectionism Affects Families

Perfectionism has some interesting aspects as it relates to family dynamics. Perfectionism manifests itself in many ways, whether it is parents or children who are perfectionists. In families where perfectionism is present, fear of judgment and criticism come into play. Family members may feel that they are always on edge against an attack. Children become consumed by their own performance, and parents must work hard to show affection and praise unrelated to a child's performance (especially academic).

If your child is a perfectionist and struggles with judging others, make sure that you as the parent address this. Belittling or constantly critiquing a parent or sibling is not a positive behavior and your child should be disciplined for treating others critically. It is important that your child learn to accept others and not hold them to the same standards to which he is holding himself. Sometimes, in addressing these symptoms of perfectionism, you are able to respond to and curb the perfectionism causing it.

Why Parents Sometimes Hurt More Than Help

Parenting a gifted child is challenging. Parents often know their child's potential and work hard to help them achieve it. It is difficult to find a balance between helping your child reach his full abilities and pushing him too hard into a lifestyle of perfectionism. Many parents will actually push their children to become perfectionists, finding mistakes intolerable. Parents who refuse to accept their child's limitations may have children who become perfectionists. Placing too much emphasis on a child's academic performance can lead to perfectionism, as well.

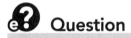 **Question**

I notice I am spending most of my time talking about school. How can I break that habit?
Parents can break the habit of too much focus on school work by taking time to engage in silly and fun family activities. Even for a gifted child, everything in life does not have to be challenging and mentally stimulating. Spend time together playing a board game, reading the comics, or watching a movie on a Friday night. Building a strong sense of family will provide your child with a foundation in who he is as a member of your family instead of an individualistic identity focused solely on his intelligence and academic performance.

Expecting exactly the same performance and abilities from your children in all areas can also cause problems. Make sure that you are recognizing each child's individual set of talents and weaknesses. Try to communicate regularly with them regarding these areas so that she knows you see her as an individual. While families may pursue group activities that everyone enjoys, it can be beneficial for siblings to be involved in different activities that allow each one an opportunity to be successful as a special member of the family.

Helping Your Child Deal
with Perfectionism

Once you have determined that your child is a perfectionist, it is important to know how to address it. You can teach your child some life skills that will help her handle the inevitable trials that come her way without succumbing to perfectionist tendencies. Teach her to not internalize her failures. Her performance is not tied to who she is as a person. Her intelligence, and how she does at school, is simply one small part of the larger picture of who she is as a complex individual. Help her see that the criticism and suggestions given to her are to help with a task, not an indictment on her. Gifted kids tend to take any kind of help or advice personally; you can help her from a young age to begin to fight that tendency.

Help your child set priorities. Certain projects are more important and are worthy of more time and effort. This is true at home and at school. You may make your bed every day, but you undo that work again every night. Perhaps hospital corners each morning before school are unreasonable when faced with the reality of the situation. The same goes for mowing the lawn. Your child can do a good job in a relatively short amount of time while perfection may take more time than the task warrants. On the other hand, leftover food on freshly washed dishes may not be acceptable. These are just a few examples of ways you can help your child see that there are some situations that call for a higher standard than others.

As a family, you can try to focus on improvement as opposed to perfection. This is particularly important for gifted children. If your child struggles at math, you can set a more abstract goal of improving her skills instead of a finite goal of expecting an A+ on every assignment, which may be unreasonable given her limitations. It is not wrong to have high expectations as a parent, as long as they are reasonable and attainable. Make sure to celebrate your child's accomplishments. Praising her honestly for a concentrated effort in an area of weakness means far more than empty praise for a task that was not challenging to complete.

Some children find great benefit in looking at the lives of those who became successful. Abraham Lincoln is a study in rising above a person's circumstances to achieve greatness, as he overcame poverty, family tragedies, and personal defeats to become a great figure in American history. Studying prominent examples like him can help your child realize that perfection is not necessarily the only path to success.

Setting a Good Example

You can set a good example for your perfectionist child. Often, a child will demonstrate perfectionist tendencies because this is what they have seen in their environment. Some parents fail to have appropriate standards for their child. A parent may want their child to get straight As in every subject, failing to take into account their child's sincere efforts in their weakness areas. It is important for parents to set and maintain reasonable expectations for their child. It is reasonable to expect your child to do well in school without expecting him to be the best in every subject.

Your child will encounter difficulties in his school career. Many gifted children become perfectionists because they do not face enough truly challenging experiences as a young child. Most tasks are easily accomplished, and a gifted youngster becomes used to succeeding with relatively little effort, which can lead to false perceptions of being perfect. As a parent, you should be watching for opportunities for your child to attempt challenging tasks from a young age. Expose him to these situations, and allow him to work through them on his own. In doing so, he will experience both success and failure as a part of growth and develop a set of coping skills for handling both. Parents who bail their children out send the message that they think their child cannot do something or do it to their standards. Simply praise your child sincerely for his efforts and discuss what he learned that will help him with future difficulties such as this one.

One additional area where you can help your perfectionist child is to teach him not to compare himself to others. Avoid the tendency to compare your children to each other; each child has their own abilities and challenges. While your child may see his areas of strength and try to compare himself, you can help by pointing out that the other child probably has times she struggles, as well. Accepting other children as they are is a powerful skill that your child can benefit from greatly over the long term.

Modeling Failure

As adults, parents can model what it looks like to fail successfully. Teach your child that failures are a part of the learning process. If you make a mistake while cooking dinner, take this teachable moment to show your child how you corrected the recipe or simply started again. Instead of becoming angry with yourself when you make a wrong turn on the way to school, try to see the positive side of finding a new way to school or seeing interesting new stores out the window. Make light of your mistakes. Some families may keep an ongoing tally of all the mistakes that they have made as a running family joke. Your child will begin to emulate your responses. The more upset you are about mistakes, the more upset your child will be, while the more adeptly you handle these upsets, the more your child will learn to be flexible and allow for mistakes.

 Alert

There seems to be a hereditary component to perfectionism, which can make it even more difficult for parents to assist their child with this problem or even see it as a problem. A parent in this situation faces the challenging task of attempting to address their own struggle while also helping their child to overcome it, as well. A parent in this situation may want to seek the help of a counselor or close friend to discuss their troubles to help their child avoid the same in the future.

Accepting Limitations

In life, every child has areas of strength and areas of growth. The key to being successful is in the ability to accurately determine what these may be with your child. Knowing where she will have to work harder and adjust her own expectations can help her appreciate the fruits of her labor and her successes. This can be a valuable component of teaching her about perfectionism. You can talk to your perfectionist child about accepting her own physical and mental limitations. While a person's limitations may be overcome with time and hard work, the difficulty in doing so should not be overlooked. Students may also find great joy in being able to highlight their strengths in contrast to their own limitations.

Once you know what perfectionism is and how to spot it in your child, you can begin to address it. You can work to teach your child coping skills to manage her perfectionism and become a well-adjusted and successful adult.

CHAPTER 17

Underachievement and the Gifted Child

While some children who are gifted have a tendency to overperform, the opposite is also true. Many gifted children fail to reach their potential for a variety of reasons and in a variety of ways. Underachievement and lack of motivation can be devastating to parents who only want their child to reach his full potential. Parents need to be watchful for early signs of underachievement, in addition to being aware of how to address a lack of motivation when they see it in their gifted child.

What Is Underachievement?

Underachievement can be defined as a child who has a high IQ or has scored very well on a cognitive abilities test, but routinely fails to perform at a level commensurate with those abilities. Gifted children can underperform by taking easy classes, doing poorly in school, or by simply not caring about their academic efforts.

Since gifted children are statistically unique to begin with, gifted underachievers being even more rare makes creating a laundry list of typical characteristics difficult. Many researchers over the years have tried, with varying degrees of success. While this list is by no means exhaustive, these are a few characteristics that some gifted children not meeting their potential may display:

- Poor self-image and lack of confidence in abilities
- Failure to set or follow goals
- Inability to persist at tasks
- Sense of inadequacy

Forms of Underachievement

Underachievement looks different in every gifted child. Just as individual children are different, so are the issues with which each child struggles. There are, however, some common categories that many children demonstrate characteristics for with regard to their lack of motivation and performance.

Fitting In

Fitting in is when a child pretends to be not as intelligent as he may be in order to make a good impression with his peers or secure a certain social standing. For boys, this may mean placing a greater emphasis on sports, leadership, and social endeavors while taking less challenging classes or pretending not to do well in challenging classes. While some boys do suffer from the pressures of fitting in, this is far less of a problem for boys than it is for girls.

For young women, usually starting in middle school and continuing through high school and college, there can be a stigma attached to being intelligent. Sometimes this is a perceived stigma, but often it is very real. Girls sense that their knowledge is not as highly valued as that of their male peers. Teachers, classmates, and others may belittle them for their smarts. While it is not always done openly, there are many subtle ways that others diminish the abilities of girls. Girls are statistically called on less in the classroom. Boys are also more commonly selected for positions of leadership within the school and the classroom. Additionally, certain behaviors like shouting out or interrupting are far more likely to be excused in boys than they would be in girls. It is not surprising that girls learn early on that to fit in and be liked they must downplay how bright they are.

While fitting in is something that matters to most children, fitting in to the point of failing to achieve takes this to new and dangerous levels that can have drastic long-term consequences for a child's self-image as well as her academic future.

Essential

Parents should be careful not to reinforce the performance stereotypes their children may be experiencing in school. Make sure to equally celebrate both your sons and your daughters—in both areas. Girls need to be encouraged in academics and boys need to be praised for their other interests.

You can work with your child once you notice that she may be trying to fit in. Many times, parents may decide to choose what classes their children take at school. By not giving your child an option of which course to take, she can't choose the easier of the courses in an attempt to fit in. Additionally, parents can make sure that academics are taking precedence over extracurricular activities. Set family rules about what a child's academic performance must be in order to participate in clubs or sports. Finally, teach your child to value the importance of making good friends who appreciate her for who she is—brains and all!

Standing Out

Another form of underachievement is that of standing out. This can take several forms. Some underachievers begin to act out. They may seek to control their circumstances and others around them. They may also purposefully break rules and act out aggressively. Finally, a student who is acting out may have trouble expressing emotions and frustrations in appropriate ways. The best way to handle a child who is acting out is to address her negative behaviors for what they are, provide corrective measures, and teach positive methods for dealing with her complex emotions.

In addition to students who act out, other students may become defiant of those in authority over them. They can have continued emotional outbreaks, refuse to take responsibility, shift blame, mentally minimize consequences, and remain resolute against any authority figure. To help a child who is struggling in this way, parents and teachers can make sure they avoid power struggles or issuing unreasonable ultimatums without proper follow through. Parents can also teach decision making along with related consequences. In addition, a parent can ignore and refuse to engage temper tantrums.

These are a few ways that students can act out as a type of underachieving. It is hard for teachers and parents to recognize that some of these behaviors are not personal, but an attempt for a child to control and relate to her giftedness, as evidenced, for example, by a fear of failure resulting in her being afraid to take risks. While giftedness can help explain these behaviors and how they are keeping a child from being successful, parents should be careful to make sure that they do not excuse these behaviors but are consistently addressing and redirecting their child when she demonstrates any unproductive or defiant coping mechanisms.

Why It's Sometimes a Symptom of Perfectionism

While it may sound odd, underachievement can be a sign of a deeper issue. For gifted children, failing to perform can be a symptom of a perfectionist. It makes perfect sense to a gifted child—if he never tries he can never fail. Your child can continue to take classes he knows he is good at, and not have to face experiences that challenge him, and thus avoid the fear of losing his identity as a "perfect" student.

This happens most often when a child is praised for his intelligence as a facet of who they are, instead of as an example of what they do. A gifted child can tell from an early age that adults like it when they perform a certain way. Parents brag about how smart a child is or continually tell friends and neighbors that their child is so bright. Children are sensitive to this, and begin to think that their acceptance is based upon their continued performance as a "smart" person. To them, this means perfection and avoiding failure.

Alert

As a parent, try to get in the practice of phrasing your praise to focus on what your child has done as opposed to who your child is. Instead of saying "You are so smart!" trying saying, "I like how you did really well on your math test." The former makes your child's acceptance conditioned on continued performance while the latter places the emphasis on how your child did on a test.

How to Address Underachievement

Once you realize your child is failing to perform at an optimum level, there are steps you can take. Many of these interventions are also helpful to have as a general family practice in order to prevent students from falling into the trap of underachievement.

A Firm Family Foundation

Children who have a strong sense of family identity are less likely to be underachievers. If the status quo in your household is that everyone does well in school, your child will be likely to continue this tradition. Letting your child know that doing well in school is simply a part of being in your family can help her feel comfortable with being smart. This is particularly true for children with siblings. While it may be more difficult for parents of only children to instill this sense in their children, it is not impossible.

Whatever your family size, take time to celebrate the achievements of all family members. Make it an exciting and interesting part of your family time together. As a family, discuss how others are doing, how the rest of the family can help them be successful, and how this helps the family as a whole to be a better family.

 **Question**

How do you help your child understand the difference between healthy and unhealthy risks?
A healthy risk can be defined as one where the potential benefit outweighs the possible harm. Taking a calculus class can result in increased knowledge and appropriate academic challenge weighed against the risk of having to work hard, give up free time, and possibly get a bad grade. On the other hand, drinking with friends yields a good time which in no way outweighs the risks of possible health consequences, loss of control, and disappointing family members. Teach your child to weigh the possible risks and benefits and to select healthy risks from the time that they start making decisions.

Healthy Risks

You should also teach your child from a young age that it is important to take healthy and reasonable risks. One common characteristic that many gifted children have is that they are afraid to take risks because they fear failure. Gifted children will often choose the safer route in order to have a more controlled outcome. As a parent, your goal is to provide a supportive push and a soft landing place as your child takes chances, makes mistakes, and learns from the process.

Reasonable Expectations

Another way to prevent and address underachievement is to set expectations for your child. All children thrive best when expectations are clear and they know how to meet them. Make your expectations known to your child. In your family, achieving mastery may be the expectation. Your child should know that he will be expected to continue working at a task until he has achieved mastery—not necessarily perfection, but a demonstrably firm grasp on the concepts being learned. This may mean that he must get Bs in school or get 70 percent of problems correct on assignments. Decide what your family feels is reasonable, and make sure your child knows what is acceptable. Then, provide all the support and encouragement that you can to help him meet those goals. This may mean eliminating or limiting outside activities, minimizing social activities, or reorganizing bedrooms and workspaces. Make success a family goal.

As a parent of a gifted child, make sure that your expectations for your child are reasonable. Nothing is more frustrating to a gifted child than working hard, knowing that failure is inevitable. At times, gifted parents get caught up in the excitement of having a bright child, and lose sight of the child's needs and abilities. Learning is a process, and there are steps to be taken as part of that process. You cannot reasonably expect your child to go from learning his alphabet to reading Henty novels in a matter of weeks—even if your friend's child did. While it is good for parents to push their children and expect great things from them, make sure that your expectations are in line with his actual abilities.

Related Consequences

If you have decided that your family expectation is for your children to receive Bs, make sure your children also know the consequences of not meeting those expectations. Consequences are tricky to navigate. The best consequences are related to the expectation, important to your child, and not cruel or unusual to the offense. Perhaps your child loses video game time until his grades are back up or your daughter misses out on social outings with girlfriends until she retakes a test. Regardless of what individual consequences your family decides on, it is important for your child to know that you are serious about your expectations and willing to back them up.

Celebrating Success

Just as a parent wants to reinforce expectations through consequences for failing to meet them, they should also want to celebrate the successes of their children. This can be simple or elaborate, depending on the nature of the success.

⊖! Alert

One family practice that children seem to enjoy is the "Red Plate Special." The family purchases a red plate. Any child who has had a special success gets to eat off the red plate, sharing with the family what the success was that warranted the red-plate occasion. Perhaps a good test grade, taking a challenging course, or attempting a new activity could be "Red Plate Special" meals for your family. Regardless of the method, take time to make achievements a family event.

Parents should remember that gifted children are traditionally more driven by intrinsic motivation (internal) than external motivation (gifts). Help your child cultivate this skill by teaching him about a healthy sense of accomplishment, which should be the greatest reward for any achievement. Avoid bribing him into maintaining certain behaviors. Offering monetary or physical compensation for performance is rarely an effective method of training your child to be a happy and accomplished individual.

Motivation and achievement are complex issues for any child, particularly a gifted child. Parents who are fighting this battle need patience and encouragement. To see true progress takes time and love. If your child continues to struggle in this area, do not be afraid to seek help from a trained counselor or other professional with experience working on this complicated issue for gifted children.

CHAPTER 18

Giftedness and the Family Dynamic

A considerable amount of research over the last several decades has been done relating to how giftedness affects families. Studies have found that siblings' IQs are usually within ten points of each other. Interestingly enough, parents' averaged IQ scores are also within ten points of their children. Whether you subscribe to the nature or the nurture argument, there is evidence suggesting that intelligence is often a family matter. While parents can find much information on schools and helping their gifted child reach her academic potential, it is harder to find information about how to function as a family with gifted children.

Nature Versus Nurture

A long-running argument in many areas of parenting and child development has been that of nature versus nurture. Does a child's biological makeup or his environment determine how he will turn out? This takes an interesting turn when it applies to giftedness. People wonder if children are gifted because they are born that way or because their environment supports them in their giftedness.

Realistically speaking, both factors contribute. As far as the nature argument goes, an intelligent person will most likely be drawn to another intelligent person for a mate simply because they have more in common. Because they are both smart people, they will most likely have bright or gifted children. But the nurture argument comes into play, as well. People who are intelligent are more likely to know about and have access to programs and activities that strengthen and help develop the talents of their children.

Parents should also note that no one can "fake" being gifted. While occasionally a gifted child is not identified through testing, it is nearly impossible to experience false positives such that a child who is not gifted is accidentally identified as gifted. This is important for parents to consider. No amount of tutoring, extracurricular activities, and drilling will make your child gifted. Children are born gifted in just the same way as they are born tall or with curly hair.

⚠ Alert

Occasionally, you will see an anomaly. A very bright child will come from parents who do not appear to have the same level of intelligence. In an ideal world, while parents may not be able to identify or provide resources for this child, the school system will recognize and address their abilities. Situations like this are why it is so important that schools test all students to make sure children with unequal resources are exposed to testing and programs.

The Poor and Minorities

Historically, poor children and children of minority status are less frequently identified. This does not mean that there are fewer minorities and poor children who are gifted; it simply means that they often do not have the same access to testing or resources that other children may have access to. In recent years, many efforts have been made to ensure that testing is not biased against minorities and that more minorities are being identified. Additionally, programs have been created to help children in impoverished areas participate in early intervention services as well as preschool programs, in hopes that the playing field can become more level at an earlier age. There is still work to be done but tremendous efforts are being made.

Family Roles

In most families, the first-born child is more likely to be identified than the second or subsequent child. This is not because other children are not gifted; they simply tend to march to their own drummer. The first child is usually a stereotypically bright child, while the second may be more artistic and abstract, which can lead parents to believe he is not gifted. If one child qualifies into a gifted program, consider testing all of your children, as it is likely they will all be gifted. Understanding the gifts and talents of each of your children can help create a harmonious family balance while staving off conflicts and jealousies.

 Fact

This remains true even for identical twins! In studies, a first-born identical twin is more likely to be identified for gifted services than the second-born twin.

In a family, roles can sometimes be complicated when a gifted child is part of the family. Gifted children are often energetic, inquisitive, and demanding. Parents can unintentionally become focused on the gifted child (or the more demanding gifted child in a family with multiple gifted children), not realizing that the family is becoming centered on that one child instead of evolving as a collective unit.

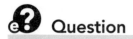

Question

How do we keep our family from revolving around our gifted child?

Children think the world revolves around them, and behave that way until their parents teach them that this is not true. Explaining the unit to whole relationship as well as the whole to unit relationship can help him visualize his place in the family. He has a responsibility as one part of a whole to make sure that the whole is functioning well. Also, as a unit within the whole, he has needs and responsibilities that are unique to him. Each of the other members of the family has these same responsibilities to balance. It is helpful to talk to your child about what he can do to support all the other members of the family as well as what tasks he can take on to help the family as a whole.

Parents can also struggle with their own relationship. A gifted child takes a lot of time and energy. Parents can feel like they have little left at the end of the day for each other after taking care of one or more demanding children all day. It is important for parents to make their own relationship a priority. Take time to go on regular dates. Your child will benefit from being around other authority figures, and you and your spouse will enjoy much needed alone time. The more you allow a gifted child to be the focus, the more attention she will seek. It can become a terrible cycle. Break that cycle early by taking the time to strengthen and grow your marriage partnership. This will also help your parenting, as you have time to discuss your children, your parenting styles, your discipline practices, and your goals for your family without your children present and outside the heat of the moment.

Handling Jealousy

In families, jealousies and resentments can be natural occurrences. Gifted children are particularly aware of differences and are always on the lookout for what they could consider unfair.

They may feel parents favor one child over another because of the amount of time and energy the family spends on that child or the attention that child receives. Whether the child's fears are valid or not, the fact that they feel them needs to be addressed.

To help avoid jealousies, make sure that your child's fears are not warranted. Be careful not to favor one child over another. Take time individually with each child to help them feel special and valued. You do not have to pay equal attention down to the minute, but try to alternate activities done with individual children. While it is important to spend individual time with each of your children, it is also good to have family activities that encourage children to learn to interact with each other and together as a whole family.

Parents may need to take the time to address habitual jealousy as a character flaw requiring training, as well. While minor instances of jealousy are a normal part of a child's social development, parents should be on guard for a child becoming characterized by jealous thoughts and actions. At its root, jealousy is a manifestation of pride. The jealous child feels as though she is not getting something that she deserves or is entitled to—most likely a parent's time or attention. Teaching children about gratitude and self-sacrifice can cause them to be less likely to feel selfish or entitled. Additionally, parents can talk to a jealous child about responding more appropriately to another family member's success and achievements with love and support instead of jealousy and spite.

Family as a Safe Haven

The world can be a scary and lonely place for a gifted child, especially in certain academic settings. Your child's home should be a safe haven where she is free of the pressures and challenges placed on her by the outside world. Home should be a place where she can get away from everything and simply be herself.

Make sure that your child has a place, or places, where she can find comfort and alone time. While every child does not need her own room, it is helpful for a gifted child to have a space where she can go to read, write, draw, and dream. This may be a closet, a room, or simply her own desk in a shared space. Some parents also have a filing cabinet where each child has a drawer to store his blueprints, drawings, and drafts. Creating these spaces shows your child she has a place within the home and that her ideas are important as well as valued.

If your family is involved in too many outside activities and rarely has time to engage in family activities at home, your child will not likely see it as a haven. Take time to evaluate all of your commitments. Make sure that the time required and potential outcome outweigh the sacrifices the other family members are making in order for the activity to continue.

 **Essential**

A good rule of thumb is to let each child be involved in one to two activities at a time. Some parents choose one while allowing the child to choose the other. Any more than this, especially for families with multiple children, can cause parents to feel more like taxi drivers and less like caregivers. You are also teaching your child an important lesson in making choices and setting priorities that will be valuable when he reaches adulthood.

Making Your Family Work Without all the Work

Everyone wants a happy and conflict-free family, but how do you do that? It can seem like a lot of work to get everything accomplished in running a household and meeting a child's need to be challenged while still having time to encourage and play with him. Families find many effective ways to do this.

Everyone Works, Everyone Plays

Having a team mentality is one way to make sure your family works effectively. No one member of the family, especially mom, should be carrying all the weight. There is nothing wrong with having chores and learning to be a part of a family. From the time your gifted child is a toddler, she can be learning to help serve within the family. If your child is old enough to play with toys, she is old enough to learn to put them away. Young children can also help put away dishes on low shelves, dust with a rag, and make their bed. Their responsibilities should grow as they do, but they should never be without tasks and duties. Doing so produces character and helps them to feel a sense of belonging and ownership in their family. You're creating a home, not a hotel with maid and room service. Additionally, learning to pick up after themselves, assist with family meals, and learn household skills prepares them for adulthood—unless you were planning on them living with your forever or renting out your services when they leave.

Children will meet your expectations. If you do not expect them to contribute and be responsible, they won't. If you expect them to clean up after themselves, help around the house, and seek opportunities to serve family members, they will. If your child is too busy with outside activities to be able to contribute to the needs of the family, you may consider whether they should cut back on those activities.

The Importance of Family Mealtime

What if someone told you that one small change could cause your child to be less likely to engage in risky behaviors (such as drinking, smoking, and using drugs), experience depression or attempt suicide, delay having sex, and do better in school. "Sign me up!" you're probably thinking. Is it some self-help seminar or DVD series to watch? It's much simpler than that. Studies have shown that these are all benefits of families eating meals together.

Fact

Ironically, families with the lowest levels of education are most likely to eat together, while families where parents have higher levels of education are less likely to share meals.

Eating dinner together as a family is not just about sharing a meal. Sharing meals is a part of parenting your children. While you teach them which fork to use, how to keep their mouth closed, and other simple acts of politeness, you are also sharing conversation and socializing your child.

 Fact

According to a *Time* magazine study, while greater than 50 percent of families with children twelve and under share at least one meal together, by the time children reach age seventeen, less than 25 percent of families still dine together. Make sure your family does not break the habit of eating together when your child needs it the most!

Many families find it difficult to share meals together. There are so many activities and events that keep even careful families busy from when they wake up in the morning till they go to bed at night. Families eat on the run—frequenting drive-thru establishments or eating standing up in the kitchen. While it may seem hard to find the time to eat together, you can do it if you commit yourself to the goal. Try to get creative. There are only seven dinners each week, but there are a total of twenty-one meals. If you can't have dinner every night because of outside activities, maybe try for breakfast. What about a picnic in the park on Saturday or Sunday? A little ingenuity and dedication to the importance of family meals can find a wealth of opportunities for sharing time together to eat.

How many times does your family eat together? Whatever that number is, set a goal to double it over the next six months. As you decrease your outside time commitments in order to increase your family meal times together, you will see great rewards in your communication with your children as well as your family bond. It may be a little awkward when you first start, but studies have shown the experience gets better over time, and the benefits to your family increase as well.

Families are the most important components of a society. Through them, new members of society are created and trained for life on their own and the creation of new family units. Parents cannot be too careful or too vigilant in protecting their family. Make sure that you are taking the necessary steps to ensure a healthy and fully functioning family. A gifted child can be a blessed addition to your family, as long as you manage your family with a little extra care and attention.

CHAPTER 19

Communicating with Your Gifted Child

As any parent of a gifted child knows, communication can be a troublesome endeavor. There are many factors of being gifted that make communicating with your child more difficult than it would be with another child who was not gifted. A parent may feel frustrated as discussions unravel into arguments and power struggles. Many parents also struggle with remaining calm as their children throw tantrums, cry, or scream when they try to talk with them. Understanding these difficulties and knowing some strategies to counteract them can make quite a difference in the parent-child relationship.

How to Talk so Your Gifted Child Hears

In a sea of voices clamoring for a child's attention amidst television, video games, and music, parents can feel as though their thoughts and comments are drowned out and their child simply cannot hear them. Parents can adopt several strategies with regard to communication that will help them be heard by their gifted child.

First and foremost, parents need to teach and model good communication practices. Make sure that you are reinforcing the proper way to communicate with your child by your own actions. There are simple considerations that everyone can use. Make sure you are facing the person you are speaking to. Maintain eye contact while you are speaking with the other person. Eliminate distractions such as television, computers, and phones when you are trying to have a conversation. Try to use "I feel" statements instead of "You always" statements. Practicing these communication techniques can set a solid foundation for successful communication with your child.

 Fact

According to both recent and historical studies, nonverbal communication is more important than verbal communication. Communications specialists have long attempted to inform people of the importance of nonverbal communication. In order for someone to believe what your gifted child is saying, it is necessary for his actions and mannerisms to confirm what his words are saying. While this does not come naturally to most gifted children because of their difficulty interpreting social cues and interactions, these skills can be learned with practice.

Children want to be respected. So much of the world ignores them, talks down to them, or treats them as if what they say does not matter. What most gifted children are looking for is someone who cares about what they have to say. Instead of responding with the typical, "Mm, hmm . . ." or "That sounds nice . . ." while trying to make dinner or pay bills, stop what you are doing. Look your child in the eyes. Listen to what she is saying and respond appropriately. If too often you respond with careless or disinterested responses, your child will learn that you are not a person she can talk to and will move on to others who will pay attention to her. You are setting patterns in the early years that will carry over into teenage and adult life. Once these patterns of communication are set, they are almost impossible to undo.

 Question

What do I do if I've already lost my opportunity to listen to my child?
All hope is not lost for those parents who have been too busy or too preoccupied to listen, and their child has stopped talking. Children are very forgiving, and most desire to have a relationship with their parents. Start by being honest with your child. Admit that you have been selfish and distracted. Ask for his forgiveness and tell them you would like to start over. You have to demonstrate over and over that you do care what your child has to say, and that you are willing to listen. With time, perseverance, and patience you will begin to rebuild your relationship with your child.

While it may seem a difficult task to incorporate into a busy day of work, taking care of the home, and caring for children, try to carve out a few minutes each day where your child will have your undivided attention. Sit down with your child and listen, really listen, to what she has to say. Exchange in a positive dialog about a topic of her choice. Building these times into your day with each of your children will help them know that you care what they have to say and that you value discussion with them.

Parents can also help their child learn to paraphrase what others have said to ensure clarity of communication. When parents are talking to their child, they can restate what their child has said both to show that they were really listening as well as to make sure they understand. Children can learn this skill as well to help minimize mixed messages or unclear conversations.

Alert

Remember that even from a very young age, your child understands the idea of sarcasm. He knows when he is being belittled or condescended to. Try to respond politely and respectfully to your child, and resist the urge that some parents have to talk down to their child. While many young children do not have a problem with this, it is a large barrier to open communication with a gifted child.

It is important to remember that although your child is very bright and may be mature in many areas, he is still, ultimately, a child. While he may have a vast reserve of knowledge and intellect to draw from in discussions, he lacks the age and experience that builds true wisdom. Your job as a parent is to be aware of his strengths and limitations, in communication and in all other areas. Don't be surprised if a perfectly rational conversation turns into tears and tantrums. That is simply the child showing through beyond his giftedness. Remain calm, reinforce that you understand how your child is feeling, and continue the discussion as best you can.

Avoiding Arguments

Too often, parents talk only when they want their children to listen. Parents talk to their children when they want them to do something like a chore around the house. They may pull a child aside and talk to him about a discipline issue. A parent might sit a child down at the kitchen table to talk to him about a school or family issue. These all have one thing in common. The parents are talking, and the children are supposed to be listening. Unfortunately, this is not a relationship. This is a one-sided dialogue that ultimately leads nowhere or to arguments.

As a parent, make sure that you are actually communicating. This involves an exchange. You talk while your child listens. You listen while your child talks. Avoid the tendency to lecture as you give directives and instructions. If there has been a behavior or discipline issue, allow your child to explain what happened. Talk together about what she has done, whether or not it is acceptable in the family, and brainstorm future alternate actions. Eliminating a child's voice is what leads to arguments and disagreements that are difficult to resolve.

Alert

As a parent, being able to remain calm is key to avoiding or disengaging heated encounters. You may need to take a break, or wait some time before having a discussion in order to make sure that you can conduct the discussion rationally and from a position of authority.

Developing a Feelings-Based Communication Style

Often, part of the difficulty in communicating with your gifted child results from the complex emotions that your child may be feeling. Gifted children experience their emotions very intensely, but rarely have a vocabulary to match the complexity of their feelings. Most children understand emotions such as sadness and anger, but few understand the intricacies behind those emotions.

As a parent, you can help your child communicate how they are feeling by giving them words to describe those feelings. Talk about the differences in types of anger—feeling mad as opposed to experiencing rage. Talk about how feeling a little melancholy is not the same as dealing with deep sorrow. Having the words to communicate exactly what they are feeling may help your child to better express and deal with those emotions.

Many young children benefit from attaching colors to their emotions, and having an emotions journal. Coloring red on a page when they are feeling angry can help them process those emotions. This is a good start to learning to discuss emotions for children who may be too young to understand complex words and feelings.

Teach your child to communicate how he is feeling. You can model this as a parent, as well. By asking questions and drawing your child out, you can begin to have discussions that use teachable moments. For example:

Mom: I see you are kicking the door. Why are you kicking the door?

Child: Because.

Mom: Because is not an answer to my question. Usually kicking the door signals you are feeling some strong emotions. Are you perhaps feeling angry or frustrated?

Child: Both.

Mom: What happened before you started kicking the door that caused you to feel this way?

Child: Big brother said that I couldn't play with him.

A parent can continue to pull out a child's emotions, and teach him the feelings as the result of actions. How a person then responds determines how they will ultimately feel about the situation. Take each opportunity you can to teach your child that emotions are a response, but they are also our responsibility. Help him to learn that through self-control and a positive attitude, he can have mastery over his feelings and move beyond them.

 **Essential**

If you need a good resource for teaching your child an emotion-based vocabulary, check out *www.feelingfacescards.com*. The colorful children's faces make it fun for children to experiment with new words for common experiences they may previously have been unable to articulate. The playful manner makes it easy for parents to tackle a potentially difficult topic. You can hang a poster on the refrigerator or use two sets of feelings cards to play "Go Fish" or "Memory" games.

Using some of these strategies to help your child cope with the intense feelings he may be experiencing can be a valuable tool in your communication toolbox.

Teaching Your Gifted Child about Communication

As you work to develop a healthy communication relationship with your gifted child, you can teach her three key components to maintaining composure while communicating with parents and others. Most gifted children can benefit from learning and mastering these three areas of communication.

Tone

Everyone knows the expression, "It's not what you say but how you say it." Tone is especially important for gifted children to learn. Gifted children in particular struggle with the quality of their voice. While they are more sensitive to certain stimuli, many gifted children have trouble processing tone and volume because of the way that their brains work.

Some gifted children have trouble controlling their volume. They are either too loud or too quiet. Directives to speak up or be quiet seem to have no effect on them, much to the frustration of their parents, teachers, and friends. This can cause problems in situations where you need your child to be able to talk at an appropriate volume level.

 **Question**

Is there a fun way to practice volume with my child?
Some parents like to play the "Quiet/Loud Game" with their children. Families pick a silly phrase to repeat. The person playing says the phrase while the other partner tells them "quieter" or "louder." The children practice going quieter and louder by increasing increments until they are as quiet or as loud as they can manage. You can take time to name these levels to make a family audio control system: church level, library level, playground level, dinner table level, or bedtime level. You can practice saying things at the designated family volume levels to help your child learn to use the appropriate volume.

Additionally, gifted children can struggle to use an appropriate tone. They might sound mad or belligerent when they don't intend to sound that way. This causes tremendous tensions with siblings and peers who find the other child to be mean or bossy because of her uncontrolled tone of voice.

 **Essential**

One way to model tone of voice is listening to audio books, especially picture books for children. When listening to the story, parents can periodically pause the recording to talk about the character's tone of voice. Your child can use their feelings vocabulary to try to describe what the character's voice is representing. Additionally, you can ask your child to try to recreate the tone of voice or to have them say what the character said in a different way. Children love to act out situations in this way.

One of the most helpful ways to teach your child about her volume and tone is to record her while she is speaking. You can make an audio of her either in the midst of a discussion or while she is playing with siblings or friends. Sometimes, hearing how she sounds can make all the difference in helping her to learn to regulate her tone of voice or her volume.

Another way parents can address this issue is by role-playing. You can tape record or videotape your role-playing as well; every child loves to be the star! Set up situations that are common for your child to experience—perhaps a play date at the park or a dinnertime discussion. Practice having a conversation and modeling tone of voice. You can take turns modeling both the good and the bad.

Bibliotherapy and children's television shows can be helpful if your child struggles with her tone of voice. Parents can check out books from the library that model appropriate and desired behaviors. Practice reading the story aloud with the appropriate tone of voice or volume for the situation. The more practice your child has, the better she will get at using the right tone of voice for each setting she is in.

Gifted children are pragmatists at heart. While it may seem harsh, many gifted children respond well to a matter-of-fact approach. Sometimes bluntly explaining to them how their tone is being perceived by others is the most effective method for behavior modification. Telling them that others think they are mean or angry when they speak in a certain tone of voice and that makes them not want to play with them is highly effective. Other children may chafe at such a straightforward statement, but gifted children find it instructive. After showing her how her tone of voice is not appropriate, you can discuss with her why. Explain to her that other children think that particular way of speaking is bossy and will not want to play with her. Teach her that others prefer when people speak to them kindly and respectfully, and that her tone is not currently conveying that to those who hear her. Gifted children like to know the how and why, and this is providing her with that information along with the skills she needs in order to be successful.

Most children learn socially acceptable communication behaviors naturally through the social cues and responses that others provide. For gifted children, this is simply not the case. Because of social and emotional developmental delays, they may not pick up on others' responses. Sometimes, they are able to see that others do not respond well, but cannot ascertain why or learn the skills they need. Parents can help their children with these areas to ensure that they are developing to their full potential in communication as well as cognitive areas.

Timing

Learning to be aware of timing is also important for having good communication skills. Parents are more likely to say no or dismiss a child when they try to talk to them in the middle of preparing for dinner or walking out the door. The same is true for children that attempt to start conversations with the teacher while she is teaching a lesson or getting ready for recess. You can teach your child to look for appropriate times to start conversations. Finding an appropriate time can be different depending on the nature of the conversation they would like have with you. In most situations, it is important for your child to learn to ask you to set aside a concentrated amount of time, and not to expect you to drop everything to have a conversation about a sleepover or a field trip. Your child can learn to make appointments for longer discussions.

Gifted children can become selfish because the world responds to them so strongly as to make them feel a special importance. This can lead them to believe they have the right to interrupt, shout out, or dominate a conversation. These are unacceptable communication patterns, and parents should not tolerate them. Failing to correct a child lets her think such behaviors are acceptable and she will continue to use these conversation-dominating strategies in other settings where they may not be tolerated as well as they are in the home. Teaching children about the timing aspect of communication helps address their selfishness as well as train them in alternate behaviors. As a parent, you may need to have a conversation, or many, with your child if you notice she is struggling with these types of behaviors in her communication. It is best to address these issues when your child is very young and first demonstrating them, but you have by no means missed your opportunity to correct this type of difficulties if your child is older.

ⓔ Alert

Gifted children are masters of manipulation. One common practice is asking parents for something while the parent is distracted, knowing the parent is likely to mumble a distracted yes. Additionally, they may attempt to play one parent against the other. Make sure that you address manipulation as the serious discipline issue that it is with strict consequences. If you fail to do so, your child will continue to manipulate you and develop communication skills that are detrimental to future success in relationships.

In the course of parenting, teachable moments do arise where you will need to drop everything in order to talk with your child. Sometimes, children who are embarrassed or nervous about a certain topic may ask about it at a time when they won't have to have their parents' full attention in order to alleviate some of the tension inherent in these topics. These may include serious issues such as sex, drugs, or peer pressure. Be sensitive to your child and make sure to capitalize on these moments, even if the timing is less than convenient. Your child may bring sensitive topics up in the car or while you are working on another project. Try to take your child's lead, then follow up on more challenging issues with later discussions that show your child you are willing and available to talk about such things, without a need for embarrassment or secrecy.

One last area with regard to timing to consider with your child is the speed of her communication. Many gifted children get excited and speak too rapidly for others to understand them. On the other end of the spectrum, some children are so wrapped up in their own thoughts that they answer other people slowly. Both of these quirks can make it difficult for others to follow their train of thought and be able to fully understand them. Parents can work with their children to practice speaking at a normal rate of speech. Tape recording and playing back a child speaking can help them see how they are struggling. Videotaping also provides a concrete demonstration of what you are trying to teach your child.

Content

The last aspect of conversation that gifted children can learn about is the content of their communication. While tone and timing are important to building healthy communication, so is content. The content of communication refers to what your gifted child is saying while they are talking with other people. Gifted children have a few issues in this area. Perhaps the most prominent is the tendency to dominate the conversation. A gifted child can become very excited about sharing her particular passion with others. She will continue to talk long beyond the interest level of the other person. You can work with your gifted child to practice talking about a specific subject for just a certain amount of time. You may set a guideline of saying perhaps five interesting facts about a topic, or speaking for only one minute.

You can also teach your child to look for signs that the other person is interested in what she is saying. She can learn to watch for the listener nodding along or asking questions to show that they are still following the conversation. Your child can learn signs of disinterest such as the other person looking away, not responding, or acting distracted. Once your child learns some of these signs, it will be easier for her to gauge how long she should talk.

Another area where gifted children struggle with regard to the content of their communication is with correcting other people. Gifted children are precise and value accuracy. They often correct other people, in both appropriate and inappropriate contexts.

While people desire to have accurate information, it would be inappropriate for a gifted child to rebuke a teacher during a lesson. Gifted children need to learn when to have self-control for the sake of preserving relationships.

Alert

A good adage to teach your gifted child is, "Even when you're right, sometimes you're wrong." While this sounds tricky, it is a helpful motto for gifted children to memorize. It means that if the cost of being right is damage to the relationship, it's more important to protect the relationship than to demonstrate being right. Once your child learns this rule of thumb, she can begin asking herself whether or not being right will hurt the relationship.

You should take time to evaluate your gifted child's heart as well. Is your child correcting someone because of a genuine love of the truth? Or is she correcting someone because she has become prideful and boastful of her knowledge? If it is the former, you can work with her to learn the right ways to correct people at appropriate times. If it is the latter, you may need to instill a brief moratorium on your child correcting people until she learns to do so with a right attitude and purpose.

Finally, gifted children often struggle in an additional area of failing to be active listeners. Gifted children tend to listen to what someone else has to say only to the point of hearing something that catches their attention and prompts a response. They can become so fixated on giving their response that they fail to listen to what the other person has to say. This can cause problems when the speaker addresses what they were going to say but the child is too wrapped in their own thoughts to be able to hear it. A behavioral trait like this should be a warning sign to parents. Besides inhibiting effective communication, it is also a demonstration of selfishness that parents need to address as a character issue.

Gifted children can learn to be active listeners. Parents can teach them to use good eye contact so they are focusing on the other person's mouth to keep them directed toward what the other person is saying. You can also teach her to nod her head in agreement with what the other person is saying, or raise her eyebrows when she doesn't understand. Sometimes, having a way to physically respond can take away the need to share a verbal response that will help your child stay more involved in the conversation.

In a group setting, parents can teach their children the "One-Time Rule." According to the One-Time Rule, any individual child should only share one time until all the other children have had a chance to share, or until one minute has passed with no one sharing. You can explain that a rule like this is based in fairness. Ask your child how she would feel if someone else asked all the good questions and she was not able to share any of her thoughts and ideas because of that other person. Gifted children understand and accept this reasoning. A rule like this helps keep a gifted child from monopolizing the conversation. It also frees her to listen to what other people are saying after she has shared her one thought. Some gifted children savor their one time of sharing to the point of not being able to share, which allows them to enjoy the entire discussion without being overly involved. The point of the One-Time Rule is not to silence gifted children or cause them to fear speaking in public. The goal is to teach them how to be effective listeners and sharers who can take part in a conversation without dominating it.

CHAPTER 20

How to Discipline Your Gifted Child

Parents of gifted children often face a special challenge when it comes to deciding how to discipline their child. A gifted child can seem mature and responsible beyond his years, and yet still requires training and correction when he demonstrates age-appropriate instances of misbehaving. Gifted children may sometimes require an alternative method of discipline, as well.

Styles of Parenting

Family support specialists agree that parents fall into four parenting categories: authoritarian, authoritative, permissive, or uninvolved. How you discipline your children will largely depend on your individual parenting style. Take time to evaluate these styles with your partner to determine which most closely suits your current parenting style, and whether or not that is your goal as parents. Most parents are a combination of several types of parenting styles, so you may have difficulty identifying just one style that fits your personal method of parenting.

Authoritarian
Authoritarian parents are concerned with order and control. They believe in one way of doing things without much variation for freedom and individuality. Some of the possible outcomes of

authoritarian parenting are children who need to be led by others and are good at following directions. They may rebel against authority later on, or they may become indecisive.

Permissive

Permissive parents are not concerned with rules, but with relationships. Permissive parents want to be friends first and foremost with their children, and fear upsetting their children or the relationship. Parents who use this parenting style provide their children with few routines and little guidance. They offer children complete, or near to complete, freedom in their decision-making and choices. Children who grow up with permissive parents lack self-control and coping mechanisms. They have trouble with authority and refuse to accept personal responsibility.

Uninvolved

Uninvolved parents are focused on themselves and not their child. They believe that children are autonomous thinkers able to make decisions with little help or assistance from others. These parents typically have their children in lots of activities or utilize nannies and day cares to assist in their parenting. Children of uninvolved parents may have trouble establishing healthy relationships, fear rejection, and fail to take risks.

Authoritative

Parents with an authoritative parenting style set rules and follow through with consequences. They provide consistent expectations and feedback for their children. Authoritative parents encourage individuality within limits, and freedom with responsibility. Children of authoritative parents grow up to become responsible and creative thinkers. They take reasonable risks, and are confident in their potential for success.

Why It's so Hard to Discipline Your Gifted Child

Gifted children's parents often express difficulty in finding an effective method of discipline for their child. According to the National Association for Gifted Children:

When it comes to discipline, it's sometimes hard to tease apart what behaviors are about being gifted, and what portion of the problem behavior is about pushing the limits, or lack of control. Discipline with a gifted child can be very exhausting. Because of this struggle, parents may tend to give up and be lax about setting consistent limits and boundaries. A bright child can really challenge an adult with their questions, compelling rationale, and relentless arguments. However, all children need the guidance of an adult in their lives. Whether or not they fight it, allowing children to always have their way is not the solution.

Parents and experts agree: gifted children are hard to discipline, but it must be done for their own good.

Why It's so Important to Discipline Your Gifted Child

Gifted children are logical by nature. From an extremely young age, they learn the concept of cause and effect. They also learn early how to manipulate others. A gifted child thinks his way is the right way, regardless of whether or not that is true. He will often lie or manipulate peers and adults without seeing that as a problem behavior but more as a means for accomplishing his end goal. Additionally, a gifted child can become argumentative and disrespectful of those in authority over him, particularly if he disagrees with them or feels more intelligent than that person. A gifted child's overexcitabilities may also cause him to react disproportionately to a situation with angry outbursts or sullen withdrawals. These demonstrations of lack of self-control must also be addressed for a child to develop conflict-resolution skills.

In addition, gifted children are struggling with the regular behavioral struggles all children go through as they learn to accept the boundaries and limitations within their environment, so you can see why it is so important for parents of gifted children to learn how to discipline them appropriately. These are all behaviors that will cause tremendous trouble in the school or work setting for a gifted child who does not learn how to manage his impulses. Giftedness explains these behaviors more fully, but it does not excuse. Parents have to find a way to discipline that acknowledges the struggles of their gifted child while still holding him accountable for right behavior and wise decision making.

What Doesn't Work

Over the years, parents may find many strategies for training their children. Some of them are positive strategies that lead to children developing into happy and well-adjusted adults. Others are less beneficial to the development of a child.

Permissiveness

In today's society, an air of permissiveness has permeated parenting. Many parents are trying to be friends with their children. They feel that interacting with their child as a peer will build a strong relationship and create open communication. In these relationships, children are often given a tremendous amount of freedom in order to make mistakes and learn from them.

Permissiveness is rarely an effective method of training for gifted children. Gifted children have a tough time interpreting social cues and interactions, so too much freedom can expose them to situations they do not understand and are unable to cope with. They can also be highly manipulative, and may take advantage of an overly permissive parenting style to beguile unsuspecting parents. In fact, child psychology studies have shown that most children, gifted or not, do not thrive in an environment like this. Children need structure and order to reach their maximum potential. Gifted children do best in an environment of clear expectations with appropriate corresponding consequences.

Yelling

In many homes, parents respond to a child's misbehavior with yelling. While it may be somewhat cathartic for a parent to be able to quickly and emotionally express how they are feeling, it is never helpful for training a child.

Parents can avoid an immediate emotional response in a few ways. After an initial incident of disobedience or a poor choice, you can ask your child to wait in her room for you to come talk to her. Another strategy is to send your arguing/disobeying/getting-out-of-control kid to the bathroom. That way you can talk to her in private, away from siblings, and it also gives you both a moment to calm down before you come to talk. This can give you a few moments to gather your thoughts, decide on a course of action, and determine a potential punishment without responding with an initial overly emotional response. You can also keep yourself from responding with anger by reminding yourself that children are supposed to make mistakes and parents are supposed to train them in those instances. This is the primary responsibility of being a parent. Your child will likely require correction for the time that she lives in your home; it is a natural and healthy part of family life. Through her mistakes and your correction, she will learn how to make wise choices as well as handle consequences for poor choices.

Reasoning

From a young age, most parents find that reasoning as a sole course of discipline is ineffective for gifted children. Simply talking about what a child has done wrong does not lead to positive behavior changes. Gifted children learn to argue with their parents when their parents are asking them to complete a task or listen to instruction. While explaining what a child did wrong is always needed, it is important for you to remain in control of the discussion so that it does not devolve into a debate or back-and-forth discourse. These instances usually lead to a frustrated parent and an undisciplined child.

🄴❗ Alert

You may be asking yourself, what does obedience look like? A good rule of thumb is that obedience is three parts: obeying right away; obeying all the way; obeying cheerfully. Children must do all three parts to demonstrate that they respect and are adhering to your authority.

You need to discuss what kind of arguing is not acceptable, especially for bright kids who may be rather full of themselves and eager to correct their parents. As parents of gifted children, you may decide not to allow your children to respond with "Why?" when asked to do something. In this situation, "Why?" is rarely a true request for information out of a desire to understand the world better—it's virtually always a request for information so that she can use that information to build a case on why she does not have to do what you've asked her to do, which is arguing, and is not acceptable. When you ask your child to clean her room, and she asks "Why?" she should be disciplined for arguing, because she knows why she needs to clean her room. There might also be times where she doesn't know the reason why you are asking her to do something, but she needs to obey anyway. Soldiers in an army may not understand why the commander says they have to march in a certain direction, but they have to obey and march. Not knowing why doesn't give someone freedom to stop and have a discussion before they obey. A good rule of thumb is to tell the child asking why, "You may ask me that after you are done obeying, and then I will be happy to explain it to you." It's shocking at times to hear the way many children respond to their parents, and that the parents allow it because their child is gifted. While giftedness may explain your child's propensity for wanting to argue, it should not be an excuse for her defiance or disobedience. It is helpful for many parents to realize that giftedness explains why your child may try to argue, but it does not excuse your child from her wrong actions. Your home environment will be a lot more peaceful (and your kids more prepared to cooperate with those in leadership over them in the future) if you insist on quick obedience without backtalk.

Question

Are there circumstances when a child might need to discuss something you have asked him to do?
You may also teach your kids the appropriate method of making an appeal. For example, if his dad tells him to clean the garage but his mother has already asked him to do the dishes, he can say, "I'm happy to obey, but there's something you might not know. May I make an appeal?" Then he can tell his father that the other parent gave him a conflicting order. Children are not allowed to use this appeal process to inform a parent of information such as "I'm tired" or "I'm right in the middle of the fourth level of this video game." An appeal applies only to reasons they are physically incapable of obeying, or when obeying would conflict with another authority.

Bribing and Begging

Many parents resort to bribing or begging their children to behave. You have seen the parents in the grocery store, offering their child a candy bar if she sits quietly through the shopping trip. You may have overheard parents appealing to their child's emotions and begging them not to shout during a play or movie.

The problem with this style of discipline is two-fold. Primarily, it puts the locus of control on the child. It is up to the child to decide whether she wants to behave or not. It makes the child into a mafia warlord, with a mentality of, "If you don't pay, I will do something terrible to you." If she chooses not to comply with her parent, she simply makes Mommy sad or does not get a candy bar. While these can be powerful motivators for some children, they rarely are for gifted children. The second problem with this style of discipline is that the child fails to learn any real consequences for her behavior. This is not training a child; it is merely managing a child. Training a child requires teaching her right and wrong behavior along with the outcome of both behaviors for the purpose of her eventual readiness to learn to live in the world at large.

Time-Outs

For most gifted children, a time-out is an invitation to disobedience for many reasons. Primarily, gifted children are rational at heart. If they want to do something, they will do it, factoring in the time-out as part of the risk associated with the behavior. They don't consider it a deterrent, merely another aspect of their action. For most gifted kids, time to sit and think is a privilege, not a consequence. Gifted kids are often happiest when left alone to their own thoughts. Additionally, gifted kids are likely to get distracted, getting up and walking away from a time-out because they simply forget they are in time-out. You may inadvertently be rewarding their bad behavior.

Time-outs are also ineffective for gifted children because of the overexcitabilities of gifted children. Gifted children already have a difficult time monitoring and managing their emotions, and a time-out is basically a parent's way of saying, "Okay, you do it all by yourself," when your child is experiencing the height of her emotional uncertainty and instability. Most gifted children who are of an age for parents to be using time-outs need more help sorting through their thoughts and emotions, and require more direction than just thinking about what they have done. Typically, they have already thought about it and may be at a loss as to how to correct or improve their behavior without strong assistance and guidance from a concerned caregiver.

 **Essential**

This is great reason to put a disobeying child in the bathroom if you need to, so that you can talk with him again in a few minutes after you or he have calmed down. There's nothing interesting to do in there. If you send him to his room, most likely he will have a great time reading or playing, and you will forget about him while you are dealing with other kids and concerns. Then a training moment has been missed, and a child has disobeyed without direction.

Strong-willed gifted children can turn a time-out into a power struggle, insisting that the parent physically restrain them in order to maintain the time-out. For a punishment to be effective, it has to leave an impression on a child. The goal is behavior modification and heart change, which are rarely the outcome of a time-out for a gifted child.

Shame

Historically, shame has been a powerful behavior motivator. There is a normal shame that a child feels when she realizes that she has misbehaved and feels badly about her choices as well as her consequences. Healthy shame keeps a child humble and motivates her toward positive change. However, there is also a shame-based parenting style that has nothing to do with healthy shame. A child misbehaves at the park and a parent hauls her over to the side of the playground and loudly berates her for a time before sending her back to play or to a bench. The child has been shamed in front of everyone there. Parents can do this at the park, in the grocery store, or at school, among other places. Shame used without any additional conversation or consequences makes a child feel badly, without every truly explaining what she did wrong. Shame is often without consequences. Sadly, most often, shame has to do with embarrassment on the part of the parent instead of a desire to correct and train a child.

🛑 Alert

If a parent realizes they have used shame-based parenting, they need to take steps to right the wrong. Admit to your child that you treated him disrespectfully and ask for his forgiveness. If another adult treated you this way, you, too, would appreciate their apology, as your child will. Admitting that you have made a mistake does not make you a bad parent; it makes you human.

If you are going to correct your child, think of how you would like to be corrected. Would you like your boss to call you out to the middle of the office and openly criticize you in front of all your coworkers? If it is not acceptable for adults, it is not acceptable for your child. When your child misbehaves in public, as she will surely do by nature of being an impulsive child, pull her aside. Speak with her privately and quietly. Let her know what she did wrong, what you expect in the future, and what the consequence will be. You may choose to have her sit on the bench or stand next to you for a time as her punishment. These are both effective and appropriate ways to handle a public misbehavior without unduly shaming your child. You may also tell her you will withhold punishment until you get home. The trick there is remembering to carry out the punishment when you get home, because it is easy to forget when you get caught up in the busy-ness of life. Your child, on the other hand, has been living in fear of punishment, but will most likely not remind you. Instead, she will realize that you forgot, and take away the message that delayed consequences mean no consequences. You can try setting a reminder on your phone or e-mailing yourself a quick note so that you make sure to address the situation at home.

What Works

While there are many ineffective discipline strategies for parents of gifted children, there are a few that have been found to be successful.

Setting Your Child Up for Success

Set up communication patterns in your relationship with your child that have success built into them. While parents should remain authority figures for their children, this does not exclude the potential for a close and communicative relationship; it merely sets the boundaries for who is in charge. Your child will need to respect and respond to authorities for the rest of his life, and part of parenting is teaching him this concept.

 **Essential**

Some parents may be asking what true obedience looks like. Obedience typically has three parts: Your child obeys you immediately, completely, and with a right attitude. Failure to do any part of these three is failure to obey. If you ask your child to come out of the street, would you want him to delay in doing that and potentially be hit by a car for not obeying immediately?

As a parent, you should avoid asking your child questions rather than giving him directions. If you want him to do something, tell him to do it. Asking him implies that he has a choice, and who is really to say that they want to go to bed at eight o'clock? Many parents get into the habit of asking their child to do something and cannot understand why their child continues to disobey them. In this instance, the child thinks he has the option of not obeying because you gave him that choice. Learn to be direct. It is not unloving or hurtful; it is an expression of your parental authority.

Parents also need to expect obedience. In a healthy parent-child relationship, a child knows that he is expected to obey and there will be consequences each and every time that he does not obey.

Clear Expectations with Appropriate Consequences

Gifted children are by nature concrete individuals. They understand actions and reactions. If they misbehave and you react a certain way, they will come to expect that as the norm. Parents need to be aware that from early toddlerhood, children are determining how their families work based on a parent's response. Children need boundaries, and they need to know what will happen when they test those boundaries. Gifted children learn from having clear expectations and the same consequences every time when those expectations are not met. Say, for example, you would like your child to get out of bed at seven in the morning, but your child continually gets out of bed earlier each morning, even though he can tell the time. Your child needs a clear expectation that seven is the time he is allowed to leave his room. The consequence for leaving his room before then is that he will go to bed a half hour early that night. Bedtime continues to move up by a half hour each subsequent time that he gets up before he is supposed to. You have a clear expectation with a clear consequence. While it may take your child a few days, he will eventually learn that you are not going to budge and he must remain in his room until the time you as the parent have determined is appropriate.

🅔❗ Alert

Gifted children have extraordinary memories. The one time that you make an exception is the one time that your child will remember. If you are going to make an allowance, make sure that it is completely necessary and not merely for the sake of convenience. It is also helpful to explain as best you can why you are making the allowance. While in theory it is nice to offer your child grace, in practice, most children, even gifted children, are not sophisticated enough thinkers to understand why you are making an exception.

Reality Discipline

Reality discipline is a theory on discipline and parenting developed by family physician Kevin Leman that has grown to become a popular method of behavior modification in many circles. The term "reality discipline" relates to discipline that is based on real-life consequences. Parents who employ reality discipline are teaching their child to think for themselves, and how to learn to be a responsible member of society. Your goal is not a happy child; a happy child is a child that always gets his own way, and everyone has seen the consequences of children raised to please only themselves. The goal of parenting is a responsible child ready to function in society. Reality discipline says that a child is accountable for his actions and must not be protected from the consequences that come from his choices. For example, some parents ask when they should stop taking homework or lunch to their children at school when they forget it. Reality discipline says on the first day of kindergarten. Your child quickly learns he will be hungry if he is not responsible for his lunch and that he will miss recess to redo homework. As long as you protect him from any consequence of his actions, he will not have any incentive to change his behavior and become responsible. While this may seem heartless, it is actually loving for a parent to begin from a young age to train children to be conscious of the real consequences of their actions.

🅔❗ Alert

Homeschooling families can find ways to use and adapt this strategy for parenting and school, as well. Many times homeschooled children have difficulty getting ready in the morning because there is not a deadline of getting on the bus or into the car. Using a reality style of discipline, you can set a time for the day where children will wear whatever they have on at that point for the rest of the day. A few trips to the grocery store or library in pajamas will get the message across better than yelling and repeated reminders ever could.

Providing Direction with Embedded Explanation

Whether it is based in curiosity or defiance, gifted children are often inquisitive. You can learn to head them off at the pass by embedding an explanation into your directions to your child. Instead of simply saying, "Put your shoes away" you may try saying, "Put your shoes in the basket so that you will know where they are when you are looking for them, and so that no one else will trip on them." Adding an explanation keeps your child from asking you why and beginning an argument resulting in the need for correction and discipline.

You can tell your child that, whenever possible, you will include the explanation with your directions. However, your children should also know that they are expected to obey without argument, whether you provide an explanation or not. Arguing should still be cause for discipline; however, it is nice to minimize those occurrences whenever possible. Children have an easier time accepting your directions when they can understand why you are giving them.

Knowing When to Change Paths

Parents should be careful not to try every new discipline fad that comes around. If something is working, stick with it. Perhaps you can find a subtle way to incorporate additional helpful ideas to an existing discipline strategy, but in general, children do not benefit from dramatic changes in the way that parents discipline them.

However, there may come a time in your parenting that you find the strategy you are using no longer works. Perhaps a style of discipline worked for your older child but is not producing the desired results with your younger child. If you find that your strategy is not working, it is okay to change paths and try something new. When you discover your discipline practices are not working, decide on how you will change your discipline, and let your child know what the new policies will be. Children thrive when they know what is expected of them and their parents empower them to be successful at meeting those expectations.

Using Your Resources

When it comes to discipline, it can seem like there are too many resources at the same time as there are no resources that really address the unique challenges in discipline that gifted parents are facing. The bookstore shelves in the parenting section are crowded with new titles promising you a brand new child in a matter of days—if not hours! Unfortunately, most parents do not have the time to read through the newest discipline fad of the moment. They want to know what works so that they can begin implementing it immediately instead of trying a handful of techniques inconsistently with little positive result.

The best thing for parents to do is become observers. Find parents who have children that behave the way you want your children to behave. Watch what their parents do, interview them, and try to emulate them. Another strategy that strong parents use is discussion. They watch what troubles other children are having, and talk through possible strategies ahead of time. Having a plan of action before you need it is a powerful tool. Your child will throw you curve balls, but the more scenarios and behaviors you have talked through and studied ahead of time the better prepared you will be for them when they inevitably come. Parents also need to remember that their partner is their greatest ally and resource. Working together and presenting a united front goes far in ensuring a successful discipline strategy. Single parents can try to draw on the help of involved family members and concerned friends for help and support, as well. If what you are trying does not seem to be working, ask friends what books and websites they like. Instead of blindly selecting a book at the library or bookstore, find out what has worked for other gifted parents in your circles. If you need to, find a caring family counselor or family support specialist who can give your family some extra help to get you back on track. Above all, consistency is your greatest resource. Faithful parents disciplining their children fairly with love will operate from a position of strength and accomplish results.

Kids need boundaries. They like boundaries, and thrive in situations where those boundaries are clearly defined, even if they will not admit it. Children who grow up with overly permissive parents, or even more serious issues in their home like alcoholism or drug abuse, often tell friends in childhood or later in adult life that they wished their parents had more rules for them. Lack of boundaries makes children feel fearful and insecure. Boundaries give children a sense that they are loved, cared for, and protected.

CHAPTER 21

Building Resiliency in Your Gifted Child

How do parents help their child develop the qualities that will cause her to be successful now and for life? As a parent, you desire both to protect your child from any potential pain but also to prepare them to handle the trials that will inevitable come their way. Resiliency is one of the early skills that you can teach that will lay a foundation for many of the later coping mechanisms your child will need to manage whatever life brings her way. By helping your children to develop the qualities they need in order to become resilient, you equip them for the challenges and difficulties that will surely come their way, so that they handle them with grace instead of being swept away by the tides of life.

What Is Resiliency?

Resiliency is the way in which a person responds to the natural changes that are a part of life. People with high levels of resilience are able to remain calm under pressure, and draw from a reservoir of skills in order to meet challenges with clarity and wisdom. People who never learn the skill of resiliency may become overwhelmed by life's troubles and unable to handle the change that may result. They may also develop unhealthy coping mechanisms that can lead to problems throughout their lifetime when challenges inevitably present themselves.

Qualities of Resilient People

Researchers who have studied resilience over the years have determined a variety of qualities that resilient people possess. Resilient people are problem solvers. They have a strong sense of self and an individual identity that gives them personal strength. In order to be resilient, a person must fully understand that life is not going to be perfect and trials are a natural part of growing as an individual. In addition, resilient people have strong emotional attachments to those around them as well as secure relationships with others.

Habits of the Mind

California State University professor Art Costa has identified sixteen characteristics of intelligent and successful people that have come to be referred to as the Habits of the Mind. By teaching these habits to your gifted child, you can help her develop a strong, resilient approach to life's challenges.

- **Persisting:** Intelligent people stick with a task until it is completed.
- **Managing impulses:** Intelligent people are not slaves to their impulses but are purposeful and take their time.
- **Listening to others with empathy and understanding:** Intelligent people respect and acknowledge the thoughts and feelings of those around them.
- **Thinking flexibly:** Intelligent people can attempt new strategies to find solutions.
- **Thinking about thinking (metacognition):** Intelligent people are reflective and spend time trying to understand their own ways of thinking and interpreting information.
- **Striving for accuracy and precision:** Intelligent people are not satisfied with things that are done in a haphazard or careless way.

- **Questioning and posing problems:** Intelligent people are always growing and learning by asking questions and trying to find problems that need solutions.
- **Applying past knowledge to new situations:** Intelligent people use their previous experiences and mistakes to help them in the future.
- **Thinking and communicating with clarity and precision:** Intelligent people make sure that their thoughts are clear and accurately presented to others.
- **Gathering data through all senses:** Intelligent people are constantly using all their physical resources to collect and sort information.
- **Creating, imagining, and innovating:** Intelligent people are not happy with the way that things have always been, but are looking for new, better, and different ways to solve problems.
- **Responding with wonderment and awe:** Intelligent people never find life routine or boring, but can always be excited by some facet of every experience.
- **Taking responsible risks:** Intelligent people are not afraid to push the limits to find new opportunities for learning and achievement.
- **Finding humor:** Intelligent people can find something entertaining and amusing in the most trivial of encounters.
- **Thinking interdependently:** Intelligent people understand that we are naturally social and look for opportunities to use the skills and talents of others for the good of their own learning.
- **Learning continuously:** Intelligent people know that learning is what the brain does, and is not dependent on a classroom setting or an academic instructor.

Parents can integrate these Habits of the Mind by posting them on the refrigerator and discussing them regularly. To the child who tells you she is bored, you can respond, "Well, intelligent people are learning continuously. What are you learning right now that you can find humor in or respond to with wonderment and awe?" Using the habits of the mind in conversation and in teaching your children promotes higher-level thinking and an advanced vocabulary. Making them a part of your everyday life is a simple way for you to help your children be responsible and learn successful behaviors for their future. You can find out more about Habits of the Mind and the work of Art Costa at *www.instituteforhabitsofmind.com.*

Why Gifted Kids Need Resiliency

Life is going to give your child lemons. He will have a choice as to whether he wants to sit around sucking the bitter fruit of life or whether he wants to find a way to turn those lemons into a sweet juice. Being resilient frees your child from being a victim of fate and enables him to take power of his life and circumstances. Children who do not learn resiliency are immobilized by trials, while living a sheltered and limited life. Developing skills to cope with adversity helps your child become a strong and empowered adult. Many gifted children are afraid to make choices for fear of the outcomes. They are content to let their parents make their decisions for them, and are more than happy to allow the majority of responsibility to fall upon their parents' shoulders. While you do need to be responsible for your child, you must also train your child for adulthood by teaching him how to respond to difficult circumstances. Learning to take responsibility can protect your child from assuming the role of the victim, or learning to shift the blame when bad things happen. Part of teaching your child to be resilient is teaching him to become responsible for his own actions and subsequent consequences. Failing to do so will keep him from being able to face trials in his adult life.

Believing the Best

An important life skill essential to developing resiliency is learning to believe the best in any situation. It is all too easy to assume the worst and decide that everyone is out to get you. A victim mentality leads to a cynical and unhappy existence for those who are unable to rise above thinking that way.

As a parent, it is critical that you model this for your child. You can demonstrate that you believe the best in the way you talk about work situations. Instead of criticizing your boss's decisions at the dinner table, you can choose to see them in the best possible light and share that with your family. Your child will respond to the authority figures in her life in the same way that you do. If you complain about and demean those in authority over you, your child will learn to do the same with teachers, coaches, and even her parents.

Take this even farther with your child by redirecting her when she falls into having a negative attitude. If she is choosing to think poorly of a friend or classmate, help her redirect her thoughts and try to find a possible solution that is not negative.

While it may seem naive to choose to see life in a positive light, a person who is able to do so has a better chance of remaining focused and happy in life. Others may act in a mean-spirited or cruel way, but a resilient person is able to rise above her experience and find the good in both the other person and the circumstance. Every person has a choice in how they respond to what happens to them: They can choose to maintain their joy and zeal for life or they can choose to become bitter and disenchanted.

Praising Efforts over Accomplishments

Advocates in the gifted community for years have been teaching parents to praise their children's efforts. This is a hard skill to master. It is simply easier and more natural to praise something that your child has done. Praising the final accomplishment minimizes the work he has put into his endeavor. In sports, if parents only praised their child when they won or were the best, there would be a vast number of unhappy children who felt like they had not succeeded. In order to build resiliency, it is important to learn to praise the process that your child has undergone. This helps him understand that success is not measured by the final product or the final grade. Not everyone is going to have a finished product that they are satisfied with at the end. Resilient people are able to appreciate the steps that were taken throughout the process as well as the end result.

ⓔ❗ Alert

Parents want their children to be the best at whatever they do, and are driven to help them succeed. Make sure that you take time to consider why this is important to you. Do you want your child to win so that you can tell others about it and feel proud? If you are not pushing your child toward a goal because you really believe that it will help him grow and become a better person later in life, you might want to reconsider your efforts and admit your personal struggles with unhealthy arrogance.

Choose Optimism

Resilient people are able to look on the bright side of life's dilemmas. Someone who is not resilient becomes crippled by troubles and wallows in a pit of despair. Whereas most people's inclination is to take on the role of the victim, a resilient optimist looks at herself as more of survivor. A resilient person finds a silver lining, picks herself up, and moves on with her life. Optimism is not natural to a person, but is a learned skill that must be demonstrated and practiced. You can help your child learn to be more optimistic by looking for the good in a seemingly difficult situation. You can help her by avoiding negative comments and modeling a positive attitude and outlook on whatever you or she may be experiencing. Children who only experience complaining and bitterness will learn to respond with the same attitude. Additionally, you can relay to her that whatever she might be going through is only temporary. Whatever the situation, there will come a day when she will be able to look back on the experience and understand how she grew as a person through the trials, no matter how pressing they seemed at the time. Share such experiences from your own life to help her see that you are able to empathize with what she is going through and to provide a model of learned optimism.

Acceptance

People who are resilient also develop an attitude of acceptance. A person's natural first response to a difficult circumstance is denial. Many people never move beyond that initial experience of denial. A resilient person is able to address what has happened with a sense of acceptance. While they would not have willingly chosen to go through this trial, they begin to accept it for what it is and acknowledge that something can be learned from going through it. Children who are accepting of what life brings them are also better able to adapt. They are not held back by the need to fight against a situation, but are able to move on and begin attempting to address whatever the difficulty is that they might be facing. Those that learn to accept the circumstances they are dealing with are able to take initiative and attack problems head on instead of withdrawing and avoiding issues.

How to Build a Firm Foundation

One of the most important ways that parents can build resiliency is to give their child a sense of belonging. In recent studies, one of the primary factors in a person's success at dealing with difficult situations was whether or not he had strong social attachments. Having strong family ties can anchor a child who would otherwise feel lost in a sea of life's storms and changing tides. As a parent, you can create these attachments by spending quality time with your child. You may decide that for the sake of building familial bonds, your family needs to refrain from outside activities for a time.

You can also help him develop strong ties to his siblings. While the friendships of school and activities come and go, siblings remain a part of a child's life. Teach your children to be friends by involving them in activities together. Help them learn conflict resolution. You may see the need to limit play dates and activities with other children in order to help your child develop stronger bonds with his siblings. While your child may rebel against this, as a parent you have to consider which relationships are most important for your child to work on given the limited amount of time that every child has for social interactions. Your child may enjoy the company of another child, but will that relationship build the lasting foundation he will need to face adversities in life, or just be a temporary source of fun and excitement?

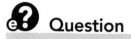 **Question**

How can I encourage my children to build a stronger relationship?
There are many ways parents can facilitate friendships between their children. Participating in family service projects together teaches children both to work together as well as to value the strengths and resources their family has. Families can read books aloud together, not just when kids are small but even through their teenage years. Your children may like to take picnics together, fly kites at the park, tour museums, and participate in shared hobbies. They can also enjoy relaxed time together as a family, simply enjoying each other's company with the television turned off.

Resilient children are exposed to a belief system that makes the world bigger than just their own experiences within their family. Children who have been exposed to a system of faith and morality understand that they are a small piece in a larger puzzle. This can promote resiliency by helping them be aware of the bigger picture in life. Their experiences do not seem to have as much significance or importance because they understand that there is more to their life than just this individual experience.

Additionally, you can aid your children in developing resilience by allowing them to fail. It may seem counter to your goals as a parent, but failure is a great teacher. As you fight the urge to protect your child from any kind of failure, you are teaching important skills that create resiliency. Your child learns that not succeeding does not debilitate him. He learns to bounce back from a difficult situation and come back even stronger than he may have previously been. Your child also learns that you will be there for him no matter what. When you protect your child from failing or solve all of his problems for him, he begins to believe that your love is conditional upon his success. He also believes he must really be incapable of handling life himself; Mommy thinks it is too dangerous for him, so she had better do it for him. Seeing that you continue to support him and cherish him even when he is not successful allows him to understand that you love him unconditionally, and will always be his support and advocate.

CHAPTER 22

Planning for the Future with Your Gifted Child

G ifted parents are often trying to stay one step ahead because of the time and energy required in planning for the future for a gifted child. Whether it is looking ahead next year or far into your child's future, it is wise to be aware of what is coming for you and your gifted child. Parents can be planning for their children in many ways. You can be looking forward to future school years and school programs. Additionally, parents can begin planning for a long-term future by helping their child evaluate college and trade programs. Parents can also introduce their children to career opportunities from a young age. All of these areas are aspects of a gifted child's future that a parent needs to be considering.

Your Child and the Short-Term Future

In terms of planning for the future, it is smart to be thinking a year or two ahead. While you may be content with how your child is learning and being challenged currently, it is important to be cognizant of changes that need to be made for her upcoming future.

Schooling
One area where parents should be thinking ahead is with regard to their child's schooling. Many parents find a program that they like where they can be happy for a number of years. Other

parents need to look ahead to the coming school year and consider what other options might be a better fit for their child. Some schools go through administrative changes that change the viability of a school for particular children. Other schools change their programming. Children grow and develop, as do their needs. A school that might have been a good fit for elementary school may not be the best place for an older child.

Parents should also keep in mind that school program placement can be very competitive. If you have a school that you would like your child to attend, it is important to make plans long before your child is of an age to attend that school. Many schools have substantial waiting lists or requirements that need to be met before your child is able to attend. Planning ahead will help make sure that you are not missing out on good opportunities for lack of foresight.

 Alert

While it is important to be proactive in making decisions about schooling for your gifted child, parents should also be wary of "school hopping," which has become an epidemic in current society. Change is difficult for gifted children, and parents should remember that no school program is going to be absolutely perfect. Before you begin changing schools each year looking for the perfect program or the perfect teacher, consider the impact that frequent school changes will have on your sensitive young student.

Parents need to keep the future in mind when they are thinking about their children. While it is important to be content with your current circumstances, planning ahead should always be in the back of your mind.

Your Child and the Long-Term Future

Just as parents are thinking ahead to next year, many are also planning ahead for their child's long-term future, including high school, college, and beyond. One important fact for parents of gifted children to remember is that they are happiest when they are pursuing something about which they are passionate. While for some children this can be done through the pursuit of a college degree, for others this may mean another path. For a gifted child, the degree is not as important as what the young person is doing with his life. You can help your child by presenting different examples of what success looks life in addition to being supportive of him regardless of his individual career path.

After High School

Parents begin helping their children plan for the future while they are still in high school, if not before. There are many steps that concerned and proactive parents can take to give their children a head start in their adult lives.

While your child is young, you can take steps to prepare him for success in college. While having a high IQ, good grades, and impressive test scores will most certainly not hurt him, there is more to getting into an excellent college than just those factors. Colleges look not just at academics, but at the whole child. They tend to look highly on students who have been involved in their community. Additionally, colleges favor students who have taken on leadership roles in the public services realm, within their high school, or in their community. These are important for many aspects of the gifted child's personality, with the added benefit of helping him look more attractive to potential universities.

A new concern in the technological age is also an individual's online persona. With social networking sites, personal blogs, and other Internet resources making the world quite small, colleges can quickly find out more about your student than you might like them to know. It is important that your child be aware of this, and from a young age maintains a respectful and responsible public facade. This will become increasingly more important as more children grow up within the global classroom and marketplace.

Choosing the Right College

Of course, parents have dreams of their children attending a prestigious Ivy League college. For many, this seems the pinnacle of a gifted child's full potential. While this is true for some gifted children, it is not necessarily a prescription for collegiate success. If your child is more shy and reserved, a large university might not be the best fit for him. Your child may benefit from attending a community college for a few years, or perhaps a smaller specialized college.

Additionally, if your child has already demonstrated a specific passion, you might be able to find a college that has a specialized program in his field of study. While a school might not be prestigious or highly ranked, a specific program within the school might be the perfect fit for your child. Try not to lock your child into MIT or Stanford without looking at his interests as well as all of the options available.

Trade Schools

For some gifted children, college may not be the best option. Bill Gates and Paul Allen were both college dropouts who went on to found Microsoft, one of the most successful software companies of all time. College may not work for your child, either. Be careful to make sure that while you encourage a lifelong love of learning, you don't limit your child's potential success to only one path. Many gifted children who are talented with building and creating find great success in attending a trade school and starting their own business. As a parent, try to recognize your child's talents and find the path that is best suited for helping him use those abilities to his maximum potential.

While it is not wrong to encourage your child to attend college, be cautious of giving him the message that there is only one path to success. The danger in this is when that one path is not the right one for the child. In the absence of the proscribed path, those children have difficulty recharting their course, and often flounder instead of being able to try a new tactic to find lasting professional success.

Careers

The problem that most children face is not in deciding what job they would like to do, but in knowing what jobs there are to choose from. Think about your child's particular talents and interests. One of the driving factors in your child's future success is in finding his passion. Some children are fortunate to know from a young age what they love. Many youngsters decide that they would like to be a doctor or a scientist, then spend their life working toward that goal. Other children need more direction. Many of the jobs that your child may do one day have yet to be invented!

 Essential

It can be helpful for children to understand the two primary philosophies on work. Some people do work that they love; others work so they can do what they love. Especially fortunate people are able to combine both; however, in most instances adults make a choice. Often, the work that you love is not necessarily the job that will support the lifestyle you like. Helping your child understand the balance between these two philosophies can assist him in making choices about what career he might be interested in.

One of the best things you can do is to introduce your child to a wide variety of adults in many professions. Seeing that they have options can be helpful to a gifted child. Try to be creative in the professionals you introduce him to, and make sure that you reinforce that maybe the job for him is something that he will one day create. As your child meets adults in varied careers, he will be able to learn how those adults made their career choice. Hopefully, your child will be able to meet adults who have a passion for what they do that will inspire him. Even if your child does share their interest, passion is contagious, and gifted children are the first to recognize an all-encompassing love of a topic or subject.

As you talk with your child about his future, be alert to decisions he may be making based on fear so that you can help him work through those fears. Many children decide from a young age that they don't like math, and quit taking challenging math classes. This limits their future options as well as teaching them to make decisions based on their feelings as opposed to using wisdom and reasoning. If your child has had a history of failing to take appropriate risks, this is something to address before it has lifelong consequences for him in his future career field.

Life

As a parent, the ultimate goal is raising a happy and well-adjusted future adult. Keeping this final goal in mind can help parents remain focused and assist in decision making. Things that seem vital and important right now may not have a lasting impact on the goal of raising a future man or woman. For gifted parents, it is easy to get caught up in the decision that you are making right now. Many parents feel as though each and every decision that they make will be the deciding factor in their child's future success. In order to stay sane, parents should try to keep some perspective. You make the best decisions you can at the time, given the knowledge you have. After that, you have to let go and allow yourself some freedom. Good things and bad things will happen to your child; some because of the choices you have made and some because of factors outside of your control. Learning to accept this and teaching your child to do so as well is just additional training for them for life. Making hard choices and coping with life's changes are facts of living that you can help your child learn to adapt to while he is still young.

Realistic Goals

Parents can give their children wings to soar while still helping them keep their roots in the ground. The goal is to find a balance between the two. When your child is younger, it may be easier to indulge her goals, but as she gets older, you want to find a balance between providing positive encouragement as well as healthy wisdom. While it may seem charming for your eight year old to be debating between careers as a lion tamer or the president, this becomes less practical approaching the high school years where plans are being made. As a parent, you can aid your child by helping her to set realistic goals. This should not minimize her dreams, because gifted children are brilliant dreamers capable of extraordinary feats. It does, however, mean that you talk through her goals and try to instruct her in planning out the steps to make those dreams become reality.

Many children in today's culture struggle with wanting to have great accomplishments but not knowing where to start. As a parent, this is where the wisdom of experience comes in, as you help your child turn those dreams into a reality.

Coping with Change

Gifted children struggle with change. This is critical for parents to be aware of concerning making plans for the future. Many gifted children find even the most trivial changes difficult, like a new type of milk or a different brand of shampoo. When considering changes like a new school or a different teacher, keep in mind that gifted children need to be prepared for such new situations.

For children who struggle with these issues, thinking about the changes that come with the future can be frightening and overwhelming. The thought of a new classroom and teacher, let alone a whole new school or completely new peer group, can lead to intense anxiety with psychosomatic consequences. As a parent, it is important to help your child learn to deal with change as a part of life from a young age. While you would not want to stress him to the point of breaking just for the sake of trying to teach him a lesson, periodically introducing changes as a course of routine can help him to develop adaptation and flexibility. One strategy some families employ is having a new meal each week on a certain day. Every Tuesday, the family tries a new recipe from a different country or culture. You can also institute a day where you make a game of trying something new or changing things around. Perhaps Friday is "Flexible Day" in your house. You try a route to school one Friday and get ready in a different order another Friday. While these are simple steps, they can give you opportunities to talk to your child about the value in being flexible and the importance of not being debilitated by a new occurrence.

Parents should not minimize the importance of conversation with their gifted child. Whenever possible, gifted kids benefit from being prepped for upcoming changes. If you know you will have a different babysitter than normal, arrange for your child to meet them ahead of time while you are there, after explaining to them why the sitter will not be your usual caregiver. Gifted children are little researchers, and the more knowledge and information they have in approaching a new situation the more powerful they will feel in handling that change. Anything you can do to give him facts to grab onto or a reason for what is happening will be of great benefit to him during a transition time period.

When it is not possible to prepare your child for changes, as sometimes is the nature of life, try to talk to him about it afterward. Discuss how he felt about what happened, what he thought he did well, and how he might be better able to handle the change in the future.

Essential

Some families have found a calming trigger for their children by having a family code word that means everything is all right. If someone new comes to pick them up from school unexpectedly, they can bring a slip of paper with the code word written on it. While parents are out at night, they can call and whisper the code word. For many children, having and hearing the code word can be like a switch that turns their anxiety off and their sense of security on.

Modeling flexibility is another strategy for helping your child deal with the difficulty of change in circumstances. If your child sees you laughing and making light of failed plans, he will learn not to worry about disruptions in routine. However, if your child sees you becoming irate over a closed freeway exit or canceled dinner reservation, he will learn that change is bad and see negative ways of handling those circumstances. If you have had difficulty with handling change in the past, fear not. While it is hard to demonstrate self-control, parents, too, can discuss with their children when they handle situations poorly and how everyone could do better the next time. Children appreciate a parent's humility and the knowledge that parents are still learning about life, as well.

Caring and Compassion

The single best tools for parents in preparing for the future are caring and compassion. It can be troublesome for anyone to think about the future with a completely calm and resolute demeanor. Try to remember back to the time you were your child's age, when you were making plans for the future or when others were making plans for you. A healthy dose of empathy can remind you to be gentle with your child and a little extra patient when she is struggling. This is especially important with older adolescents. It can often seem as though they put off making decisions until the absolute last possible moment, or even delay until decisions are made for them based on their own indecisiveness. This is a popular coping strategy for many gifted children. Procrastination or boomerang consequences take the hard part of making decisions out of their hands. Be careful not to let your child become a prisoner of circumstances or to feel like a victim. As the parent, you must delicately balance the dispensing of wisdom and firm direction with the tenderness and grace of a loving caregiver.

CHAPTER 23

Community and Political Involvement for Parents of Gifted Kids

One key way for parents to give their child a better experience of being gifted is to get involved. Parents can build positive relationships at the same time as they are advocating for change by participating in movements that work to make a difference for gifted children. While the gifted community is by necessity small (only 5 percent of parents, just as gifted kids are only 5 percent of the student population), together, even that small group of parents can push for change at an individual, community, and national level.

Change at the Individual Level

Parents can begin advocating for change for their own individual child. Within your child's classroom, you can be an advocate for change. You can provide your teacher with books and resources on giftedness. Let the teacher know about guest speakers coming to your area, new websites, or current research in the field of gifted education.

You can also provide aid in your child's classroom to help the teacher better meet the needs of the gifted students. In speaking with many gifted teachers, there are several specific ways that parents can be most helpful. Parents can provide supplies—many schools have inadequate funding for supplies and resources that are needed to challenge gifted children. You and your family can donate items that are necessary to ensure your child gets the learning opportunities he needs. Teachers, like parents, are also limited by only having two hands. There is only so much one person can do in a given amount of time—a parent can help by volunteering to come in and provide assistance in the classroom. Parents with flexible schedules can offer to help with reading groups, one-on-one tutoring, or project preparation. Parents with less flexible schedules can lead a science experiment, present a guest lecture on their career, or prepare supplies at home for in-class projects. While not all teachers are receptive, you can do everything you can to make sure that your child's learning environment is the best it possibly can be for the time he is there.

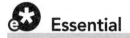 **Essential**

It is important to avoid getting off on the wrong foot with your child's teacher. Remember, most parents think their children are gifted, and you are probably not the first person coming to the teacher asking for change. If you try to remain positive, avoid accusing, and listen to what the teacher has to say, you are more likely to get the results you want. Come with a plan of action, having carefully considered what you will say to avoid emotionally charged encounters.

Change Amongst Parenting Peers

Many parents of gifted children feel helpless and alone. Becoming involved in your child's school or with your school district's gifted program can help. Where previously you were one voice in a sea of many speaking for change, now you can join together with other parents to have a real voice. Parents can start at their own school by attending meetings of the school's parent organizations. As you meet other parents, you may find others who have gifted children as well, while others may become friends who you can teach about giftedness in order to correct inaccurate stereotypes. Regardless of how much you have in common with the parents you meet, you are building a network of other parents who can help you speak out for change and adequate programming for your children's needs. Administrators and teachers may be more willing to listen to a small group of parents than they were to listen to just one individual parent.

As a parent, you can advocate for change amongst other parents. Many parents inside and outside of the gifted community are still unaware of what it truly means to be gifted. Families can be confused in much the same way you might have been when you first heard about your child being gifted. Knowledge is power, and gifted parents have the responsibility to share what they know with other parents. If you know parents who are confused or have wrong information about giftedness, provide them with information, articles, and books to change their thinking. This may be as simple as a conversation at the bus stop or as complex as offering to read through a book with them. You can decide how you best want to handle these situations, and how to be the most support to another parent.

Question

Where do I start if I want to form my own parent group?
You can start by learning as much as you can about gifted children and the gifted community in your area. Try to read the current publications on gifted education. Post flyers at your school and at other local schools. You can ask the local gifted services coordinator to let other parents know about your group. As you begin meeting with other parents, find an agenda and program structure that works for all the parents there.

You can take some steps to provide knowledge to other parents in your community. You might try working with a local parent group to host a book discussion or round table on issues in gifted education. Become involved with your local gifted organization or start a parents' group with parenting peers at your school. This can be informal: a group of moms having coffee once a week while the kids are at school or an activity. It can be a formal group with members, officers, and an agenda. Each group is tailored to its members. Some parents also enjoy online message boards where they can share parenting strategies and find a safe haven for talking about their gifted child. However you decide to get involved with other parents, remember that the goal is collaboration not competition. Try to keep in mind that you are working together with these parents to create the best learning environment for all gifted kids, and not competing against them for whose child is the most gifted.

Remember that the stereotypes discussed regarding gifted education are still alive and well in your community today. Other parents may view you as elitists or snobs, but you can persevere. Change begins small, one person at a time. As you seek to raise your gifted child into a kind, well-adjusted person, others will begin to notice and attitudes may begin to change. You can be a positive voice against the myths, helping to enlighten others along the way.

Change at the School Level

In most areas, schools are organized intro districts. Districts are run by school boards, which are formed by concerned community members elected to the board for a predetermined amount of time. Most are local business people or concerned parents such as yourself. They serve full-time jobs outside of their volunteer board service.

The majority of decisions regarding programming, funding, and resources are made by the school board. As a parent, you can advocate for your gifted child by becoming involved in the workings of your school district's governing board. You can get to know the members of the governing board. Offer to take one or two out for a cup of coffee to get to know them better, and to learn why they ran for office. As you get to know them, you can begin to advocate for your own child and for gifted programming. If the school board members are not familiar, they may be unaware of how inadequate the funding or programs might be for gifted students in your school district. You can provide them with information to help promote change at the district level for gifted students.

You can start out by attending board meetings. Agendas are usually available ahead of time. Attending the school board meetings will give you powerful insight into how decisions are made at your schools. You can use this information to try to promote changes within your school district. If you would like to become further involved, consider running for office on the local school board or encouraging another gifted parent to do so. You might also consider serving on a committee or volunteering with a bond election. The more people you know within your child's school district, the better bargaining tools you will have when you need them. Keep yourself from being just another nameless face by becoming involved. While you may not care about the committees you are serving on or the jobs you are doing to help the school board, you are building a team of allies and collaborators for when the time comes.

Change at the Local Level

Your state's gifted organization is an excellent resource for information on giftedness at the local level. You can find information there on what current laws and funding are in place, the changes lawmakers may be working on, and ways to become involved. Most state gifted organizations are listed through the National Association for Gifted Children (*www.nagc.org*). Through them, you can find state and city groups to get involved with near you. These groups can give you another wealth of resources and friends. In addition, they can help you to learn how state-level laws are made as well as how funds are allocated. Together, you can find out what changes are being made at a state level. You can call legislators, pass petitions, and try to get new laws instituted to benefit gifted students. Working with these local groups, you can join in advocating for new policies and procedures for gifted students by contacting state elected officials, newspapers, and other community groups who might be able to get involved in making changes to benefit gifted students throughout your city and state.

While you can contact state legislators on your own, it is often helpful to address them as a member of a larger organization. Additionally, your state's gifted organization is familiar with what is currently taking place in the legislature, and you may be most successful by advocating for gifted education through their organization. Keep in mind that by working together with them, you can all accomplish more to benefit gifted students.

Change at the National Level

While many aspects of education are determined by local school boards and state governments, the National Board of Education and the Federal Government retain a certain level of involvement in the education of gifted students. The passing of No Child Left Behind, for example, had many provisions that while not directly relating to gifted students, had tremendous ripple effects within school districts that changed some aspects of gifted education. One part of No Child Left Behind included funding for the Javits Act, which authorizes research on gifted children and gifted education. Additionally, No Child Left Behind gave a specific definition of what it means to be gifted. No Child Left Behind also coined the phrase "adequate yearly progress," which also helps those in the gifted program advocate for the necessary curriculum changes that their child needs in order to secure a year's worth of educational growth. These are a few examples of how laws that are passed can directly and indirectly affect gifted students.

Parents who are already advocating at the individual, local, and state levels can also begin to get involved at the national level. This begins with being an informed voter. Know the candidates in your area, and familiarize yourself with their policies on education. Contact legislators and find out their position on gifted education. Just as you can do with local teachers and state elected officials, you can also provide information and try to influence the thoughts and beliefs of those elected people representing you at a national level. Perhaps you can organize a group of parents to write letters or call legislators. This is especially important if new laws are coming to a vote. Make sure that you are aware of what is going on within the political context of gifted education in addition to what is going on in your own child's life. Legislators that are in favor of making changes in education will be glad to have more allies. They may call on parents to help them promote their plans and speak out within the community to gain support. A legislator's job is to present the will of the people, and your job is helping them know that the people care and are concerned about education in general and gifted education specifically.

 Essential

Confused about where to start? Try these national advocacy groups: The Council for Exceptional Children, *www.cec.sped.org*; The Gifted Child Society, *www.gifted.org*; and The National Association for Gifted Children, *www.nagc.org*.

The more involved gifted parents get, the more change will take place. The population of gifted children and parents is very small. In order for their voices to be heard, parents need to join together to affect change. While just a few parents may be able to work together to get changes at a school or local level, more parents will be needed to make sure changes are made at the state and national levels. You can have a part in this exciting work. Gifted education would not be where it is today without the hard work and dedication of parents fighting for change. You can be a part of making the future even better and brighter for gifted children.

Frequently Asked Questions

How do I make sure my child is challenged academically?

Just because your child says he is bored doesn't make it so. Many gifted children use the word "bored" because they do not have an extensive enough vocabulary to describe what they are feeling, and using the word bored typically stirs parents of gifted children to action. If you think your child might be unchallenged, look for additional signs. Students who are not being challenged tend to either become discipline problems or seek out intellectual stimulation on their own. If your child is able to read several books in the classroom in a week, he may not be receiving challenging enough classwork. If your child's teacher is contacting you about him being a distraction to other students or being disruptive, he might not be getting challenged. Parents can check to make sure their children are being challenged academically by regularly checking their schoolwork and being involved in their classroom.

When checking your child's work, look for routine or repetitive tasks. If you are making these types of observations, you may need to meet with your child's teacher or an administrator so that they are aware of your child's growing needs. Some parents decide to provide that additional enrichment at home. You can give your child research projects, invest in stimulating computer curriculum, take on family projects, or read thought-provoking literature together.

How are gifted children identified?

Gifted children are identified a number of ways. Primarily, someone observes behavior or skills in a child that suggests that they may be a candidate for a gifted program or services. Once children have been visually identified, they are tested.

Children are tested through a variety of measures. Some children are tested in a group setting while other children are tested individually. Many tests are administered by a school or gifted program; others are sought out by test proctors or local psychologists.

Tests study either a child's achievement or a child's cognitive abilities. The scores on these tests are evaluated to determine whether or not a child is clinically gifted.

If you think your child would benefit from gifted testing, you can start by contacting your school district's gifted coordinator. Most schools test all students at some point in their school career, but most offer additional testing occasionally throughout the school year. If this is not an option, you can contact a psychologist or testing organization to see about having an individual assessment done.

What are the early signs of giftedness?

The very young and gifted demonstrated some specific behavioral indicators well before children have reached a testable age. A gifted child may either speak very early or speak much later but speak in full sentences. Gifted children also tend to reach developmental milestones earlier than other children. Young gifted children appear alert, and seem to require less sleep than other infants their age. Highly gifted toddlers show an early interest in numbers and letters, many times teaching themselves to read before they are school age. They are concerned with how things work, and never seem to outgrow the stage of asking, "Why?" Gifted children may also be able to distinguish the difference between fantasy and reality from a young age.

How can I establish a good rapport with my child's teacher and school?

Parents can develop a good relationship with teachers in a variety of ways. Begin by being a positive support for the teacher at home, trying not to criticize or say negative things about the teacher in front of your child. Offer to provide aid in the classroom either by volunteering or donating supplies. Communicate openly and respectfully with the teacher in person and through e-mail communications. Don't try to have a conference with the teacher while you are dropping your child off or picking them up. Schedule an appointment with the teacher so that you have her full attention and you are not blind-siding her while she is busy trying to teach or prepare for the day. Make sure that you have documented examples of what you would like to share with the teacher, either notes about instances or work samples. Try to discuss both positive and negative elements with the teacher, and avoid contacting your child's teacher only to complain. Approach parent-teacher conferences with an open mind, with praises for your child's successes, constructive ideas for change, and a partnership mentality. Taking these steps will ensure an open and effective relationship with a classroom teacher.

Why should I have my child tested?

The primary reason many parents have their child tested is because they feel their child's learning needs are not being met. Parents have their child tested in order to receive information that can help their child have a more successful and better-suited educational plan. The results are something parents can take to a child's teacher or school in hopes of securing support services or qualifying for a special program. All parents want their children to reach their maximum potential. Testing early helps parents give their child the support and skills they need as soon as possible to give them every hope of reaching their true intellectual capability.

Parents may choose to test for other reasons, as well. Some parents suspect their child may also have a learning disorder for which their intelligence is compensating. Testing brings to light both areas of strength as well as areas of weakness, which can then be addressed.

Many parents want to know how to best meet the needs of their child. Testing gives them a fuller picture of who their child is as a learner, and helps them better understand how to teach and challenge them.

Some parents have their children tested because they want to prove something. This is perhaps the least beneficial reason for having your child tested. Giftedness is not a competition between parents as to whose child is the best and the brightest. Gifted children are special learners who deserve to be treated with respect and consideration, as their teachers and caregivers work together to make sure they are receiving the best education possible given their specific needs.

Why is raising a gifted child so hard?

Gifted children are very intense. They have many different and complex needs that are unlike those of students who are not gifted. The brain of a gifted child is always working—asking questions, posing problems, and constantly wondering. Parents are often on the receiving end of this intense scrutiny of life. Add to that the fact that gifted children experience life hypersensitively, and you have one exhausting child. Parents can remember that they are trying to do the best that they can, take time to unwind, and remember that all parents have good days and bad days. Set healthy boundaries for your child to keep them from becoming the focus of the family, and you will help yourself survive having such a potentially demanding youngster.

How do I know if a gifted program is a good fit for my child?

Parents often struggle with wondering if they are making the right choices for their gifted child, particularly with school. To check to see if your child is in a positive learning environment, ask yourself a few questions. Is my child excited about going to school? Does my child share openly (or with some prodding) about what he is learning at school? Are the teachers openly communicative about classroom occurrences and their philosophies on meeting student needs? Is my child happy and well adjusted to the school environment? While your child may not answer affirmatively to all of these, if you get primarily positive answers you are probably in a good school setting. Keep in mind that no school program is perfect, but if your child is mostly happy along with receiving appropriately challenging coursework, you can consider yourself quite fortunate.

Veteran parents will tell you that you have some teachers who you think are good only to find out later that they were not while at the same time you will have teachers you don't like who your child learned a great deal from.

Warning signs that a child may not be in a good school setting include your child complaining of frequent upset stomachs or headaches when it is time to leave for school, bringing home work that is repetitive from that year or previous years, or failure to communicate and provide support to parents from the administration. If you are experiencing any of these challenges, you may need to consider an alternative placement for your child for future schooling.

How can I make sure my child receives all the services he needs?

Parents are often their child's only advocate. If your child has special needs that you feel he is not receiving, you are his primary line of defense. The best way to ensure he is getting those services is to meet with school officials and teachers regularly. Try to be involved as best you can in his day-to-day school experiences, and ask for frequent progress reports. Make sure that his services reports and tests are kept up to date.

You may need to seek outside testing or support services if your school system is not providing well enough or fast enough for your child's optimum academic growth. Parents with children of special needs have to learn to be an advocate for their child, respectfully and patiently persevering in obtaining the necessary services their child not only needs but deserves. Remember, that if you won't fight for your child, who else will?

Recommended Resources by Topic

General Giftedness

The following are some resources parents may find helpful in expanding their knowledge on gifted education. They include resources on multiple intelligences and other topics related to giftedness covered in this book.

Eight Ways of Knowing: Teaching for Multiple Intelligence, 3rd ed. David Lazear (Palantine, IL: Skylight Publishing, 1998).

Growing Up Gifted: Developing the Potential of Children at Home and at School, 6th ed. B. Clark (New York: Prentice Hall, 2001).

Helping Gifted Children Soar: A Practical Guide for Parents and Teachers. Carol A. Strip with Gretchen Hirsch (Scottsdale, AZ: Gifted Psychology Press, 2000).

Intelligences Reframed: Multiple Intelligences for the 21st Century. Howard Gardner (New York: Basic Books, 2000).

Keys to Parenting the Gifted Child. Sylvia Rimm (Hauppage, NY: Barron's Education Services, 1994).

NATIONAL ASSOCIATION FOR GIFTED CHILDREN (NAGC)

NAGC is a support group for gifted children and parents with a wealth of information on virtually every issue relating to giftedness.

www.nagc.org

EDUCATIONAL TESTING SERVICES TESTLINK

This website is a compilation of all of the educational and psychological tests available for gifted students.

www.ets.org

Gender Issues

Parents interested in learning more about how to address the unique needs of gifted boys and girls will find these resources useful.

See Jane Win for Girls: A Smart Girl's Guide to Success. S. R. Rimm (Minneapolis, MN: Free Spirit Publishing, 2003).

Smart Boys: Talent, Manhood, and the Search for Meaning. B. A. Kerr and S. J. Cohen (Scottsdale, AZ: Great Potential Press, 2001).

Smart Girls: A New Psychology for Girls, Women and Giftedness, Revised Edition. B. A. Kerr (Scottsdale, AZ: Great Potential Press, 1997).

NATIONAL WOMEN'S HISTORY PROJECT

This site has a compilation of stories of women from all different cultures and economic classes, as well as an index of other resources.

www.nwhp.org

Perfectionism

Perfectionism is a complex issue many gifted children face. If your child struggles with this problem, check out some of the resources below that are focused on addressing and helping children as well as adults who are battling perfectionism.

Freeing Our Families from Perfectionism. Thomas S. Greenspan, PhD (Minneapolis, MN: Free Spirit Publishing, 2002).

Perfectionism: What's Bad about Being Too Good? M. Adderholdt and J. Goldberg (Minneapolis, MN: Free Spirit Publishing, 1999).

Social and Emotional Issues

The social and emotional issues relating to being gifted are vast. The resources below will help you to better understand the difficulties your child has and to develop strategies for addressing them so that your child can become healthy and well adjusted.

Living with Intensity: Understanding the Sensitivity, Excitability and Emotional Development of Gifted Children and Adults. Susan Daniels and Michael M. Piechowski (Scottsdale, AZ: Great Potential Press, 2008).

Parenting Gifted Kids: Tips for Raising Happy and Successful Children. J. Delisle (Waco, TX: Prufrock Press, 2006).

The Social and Emotional Lives of Gifted Children: Understanding and Guiding Their Development. T. Cross (Waco, TX: Prufrock Press, 2005).

When Gifted Kids Don't Have All the Answers: How to Meet Their Social and Emotional Needs. J. Delisle and J. Galbraith (Minneapolis, MN: Free Spirit Publishing, 2002).

SUPPORTING THE EMOTIONAL NEEDS OF THE GIFTED

This website has articles, webinars, and other resources for parents on the emotional needs of gifted students.

www.sengifted.org

Twice-Exceptional Students

If you are a parent to a special needs student or a twice-exceptional student, you are probably looking for more assistance in fully understanding and meeting the unique parenting needs of your child. Here are a few books that specifically address those children in this category.

Asperger's Syndrome: A Guide for Parents and Professionals. T. Attwood (London: Jessica Kingsley, 1998).

Misdiagnosis and Dual Diagnoses of Gifted Children and Adults: ADHD, Bipolar, OCD, Asperger's, Depression, and Other Disorders. J. Webb, E. R. Amend, N. E. Webb, J. Goerss, P. Beljan, and F. R. Olenchak (Scottsdale, AZ: Great Potential Press, 2005).

To Be Gifted and Learning Disabled: Strategies for Helping Bright Students with LD, ADHD, and More. S. M. Baum and S. V. Owen (Storrs, CT: Creative Learning Press, 2004).

Uniquely Gifted: Identifying and Meeting the Needs of the Twice Exceptional Student. Kiesa Kay (Gilsum: NH, Avocus Publishing, 2000).

Why Bright Kids Get Poor Grades and What You Can Do About It. Sylvia Rimm (New York: Crown Publishing, 1996).

School Options

Parents of gifted children struggle to try to make the best decision possible with regard to schooling their children. While each child and each family is different in their educational needs, knowing your options can help you to make an informed decision that the whole family can accept. Check out some of these resources for more information on what school options work for different families.

Creative Homeschooling for Gifted Children: A Resource Guide for Smart Families. L. Rivero (Scottsdale, AZ: Great Potential Press, 2002).

Teaching Gifted Kids in the Regular Classroom, Revised, Expanded, Updated Edition. Susan Winebrenner (Minneapolis, MN: Free Spirit Publishing, 2001).

Teaching Young Gifted Children in the Regular Classroom. Joan Franklin Smutny, Sally Yahnke Walker, and Elizabeth A. Meckstroth (Minneapolis, MN: Free Spirit Publishing, 1997).

The Complete Guide to Home Schooling. John and Kathy Perry (Los Angeles: Lowell House, 2000).

NATIONAL CENTER FOR HOME EDUCATION

This organization is part of the Home School Legal Defense Association and provides resources for homeschooling families.

http://nche.hslda.org

Further Parenting Resources

The following books are additional parenting resources that address some of the issues raised. Parents who would like to know more can investigate some of these resources for more information on the subject of parenting gifted children.

Helping Gifted Children Soar: A Practical Guide for Parents and Teachers. C. A. Strip and G. Hirsch (Scottsdale, AZ: Great Potential Press, 2001).

Kids, Parents, and Power Struggles: Winning for a Lifetime. Mary Sheedy Kurcinka (New York: HarperCollins, 2000).

Parent Education: Parents as Partners. Dorothy Knopper (Boulder, CO: Open Space Communications, 1997).

A Parent's Guide to Gifted Children. J. Webb, J. Gore, E. Amend, and A. DeVries (Scottsdale, AZ: Great Potential Press, 2007).

The Parent's Handbook. Don Dinkmeyer Sr., Gary D. McKay, and Don Dinkmeyer Jr. (Circle Pines, MN: American Guidance Service, 1997).

Parents in Charge: Setting Healthy, Loving Boundaries for You and Your Child. D. Chidekel (New York: Citadel, 2003).

Raising Your Spirited Child: A Guide for Parents Whose Child is More Intense, Sensitive, Perceptive, Persistent, Energetic. Mary Sheedy Kurcinka (New York: Harper Collins, 1992).

Siblings without Rivalry: How to Help Your Children Live Together So You Can Live, Too. A. Faber and E. Mazlish (New York: Avon Books, 1988).

The Survival Guide for Gifted Parents: How to Understand, Live With, and Stick Up for Your Gifted Child, Revised Edition. S. Y. Walker, PhD (Minneapolis, MN: Free Spirit Publishing, 2002).

GIFTED CHILDREN MONTHLY

This is an online newsletter as well as a database of past articles. Parents can also use this site for meeting other gifted parents. There is a nominal annual membership fee of $10 per year.

www.gifted-children.com

GT WORLD

GT World is an online networking site where parents can meet and collaborate with other gifted parents.

www.gtworld.org

HOAGIES' GIFTED EDUCATION

A longtime resource for gifted parents, Hoagies' is a comprehensive database of articles and resources for gifted parents.

www.hoagiesgifted.org

TAG FAMILY NETWORK

TAG is an organization by and for gifted parents with links and resources to help gifted parents in a variety of areas.

www.tagfam.org

Other Great Resources

These are a few resources that gifted families have enjoyed that don't fit into the other categories of resources. Your family is sure to enjoy and benefit from them, too.

Cradles of Eminence: Childhoods of More Than Four Hundred Famous Men and Women, 2nd ed. V. Goertzel, M. G. Goertzel, T. G. Goertzel, and A. M. W. Hansen (Scottsdale, AZ: Great Potential Press, 2004).

Some of My Best Friends Are Books: Guiding Gifted Readers from Preschool to High School, 2nd ed. J. W. Halstead (Scottsdale, AZ: Great Potential Press, 2001).

Way to Be: Manners. Carrie Finn (Mankato, MN: Picture Window Books, 2007).

Index

We Have

EVERYTHING®

on Anything!

With more than 19 million copies sold, the Everything® series has become one of America's favorite resources for solving problems, learning new skills, and organizing lives. Our brand is not only recognizable—it's also welcomed.

The series is a hand-in-hand partner for people who are ready to tackle new subjects—like you!

For more information on the Everything® series, please visit *www.adamsmedia.com*.

The Everything® list spans a wide range of subjects, with more than 500 titles covering 25 different categories:

Business	History	Reference
Careers	Home Improvement	Religion
Children's Storybooks	Everything Kids	Self-Help
Computers	Languages	Sports & Fitness
Cooking	Music	Travel
Crafts and Hobbies	New Age	Wedding
Education/Schools	Parenting	Writing
Games and Puzzles	Personal Finance	
Health	Pets	